The Instant
Survivor

The Instant Survivor

Survivor

RIGHT WAYS to RESPOND
WHEN THINGS GO WRONG

JIM MOORHEAD

A 4-STEP SYSTEM for CONQUERING
PROFESSIONAL and PERSONAL CRISES

GREENLEAF
BOOK GROUP PRESS

For any personal matters or issues involving company employees, supervisors and managers are encouraged to utilize appropriate resources such as employee assistance programs and to consult with their company's human resources and/or legal departments.

Published by Greenleaf Book Group Press
Austin, Texas
www.gbgpress.com

Distributed by Greenleaf Book Group LLC

For ordering information or special discounts for bulk purchases, please contact Greenleaf Book Group LLC at PO Box 91869, Austin, TX 78709, 512.891.6100.

Design and composition by Greenleaf Book Group LLC and Alex Head
Cover design by Greenleaf Book Group LLC

Publisher s Cataloging-in-Publication Data
(Prepared by The Donohue Group, Inc.)
Moorhead, Jim.
    The Instant Survivor: right ways to respond when things go wrong / Jim Moorhead. — 1st ed.
    p. ; cm.
    "A 4-step system for conquering professional and personal crises."
    Includes bibliographical references.
    ISBN: 978-1-60832-244-2
    1. Crisis management—Psychological aspects. 2. Crisis management—Psychological aspects—Anecdotes. 3. Life change events—Psychological aspects. 4. Life change events—Psychological aspects—Anecdotes. 5. Employees—Counseling of. 6. Employees—Counseling of—Anecdotes. I. Title.
HF5549.5.C8 M66 2012
658.314/5   2011932971

Part of the Tree Neutral® program, which offsets the number of trees consumed in the production and printing of this book by taking proactive steps, such as planting trees in direct proportion to the number of trees used: www.treeneutral.com

Printed in the United States of America on acid-free paper

12 13 14 15 16   10 9 8 7 6 5 4 3 2 1

TreeNeutral®

First Edition

CONTENTS

STEP FOUR. SAVE YOUR FUTURE

INTRODUCTION

HEAD-IN-THE-SAND DISTRESS TO HEAD-HELD-HIGH SUCCESS

Close your eyes and think about your company. See your colleagues sitting in their cubicles and offices. Do you know how many of your coworkers are in pain right now? Consider the range of troubles your fellow employees, and perhaps you, confront in your personal and professional lives.

Fading marriages, sick children, and faltering parents. Stagnant salaries and poor advancement prospects. Troublesome medical test results. Challenging mortgage payments; retirement, a mirage.

Why do you and your colleagues struggle when your company has robust human relations (HR) and employee assistance programs (EAP)? Because most of us don't take advantage of HR programs or an EAP no matter what trouble we're facing.

Yet we aren't equipped to resolve personal and professional crises on our own. Our parents didn't show us how, our schools never taught us, and our companies don't train us. Unable to conquer life's disasters, we suffer in silence and, too often, solo.

I know this from personal experience. Two weeks before I was to start work with a major New York company, my father died from lung cancer. He was sixty-three. A few of my new coworkers knew about this, but their focus understandably was elsewhere. So day after day I hid my sadness, clenched my jaw, and pretended I was all there. Yet most of me was with him—and my own grief over losing a loving and inspirational father so young. My wounds were invisible, ignored, and untreated. Before time eventually healed them, I did my job without flair, without passion, and without really being engaged. Similar scenarios play out among workers in every company every day.

Crises rip up families, short-circuit relationships, and disrupt companies. Haven't you encountered zombies in your workplace? Some go to work to escape reality—trouble at home. Others "phone in" assignments, skip out early, and force others to cover for them.

A Country in Crisis

The Grief Recovery Institute, a nonprofit educational institute, has calculated the cost of the hidden grief that employees bear. Factoring in divorce, money troubles, and other family burdens, the institute finds that these problems cost U.S. businesses over $75 billion a year in reduced productivity, increased errors, and accidents. "When your heart is broken, your head doesn't work right," says Russell Friedman, the institute's codirector.[1]

The economic downturn makes it tougher on employees already facing trouble. Let's take the national pulse. The divorce rate has declined slightly, but experts say it's because some couples who want to split can't afford to do so. Depressed home values and disappearing jobs trap couples at odds in fractured marriages. A husband and wife in suburban Maryland who want to call it quits told the *Washington Post* that they continue to share the house they hope to sell: he's in the basement, she's upstairs.[2]

According to a recent report by the National Alliance for Caregiving and AARP, the number of Americans looking after someone fifty or older jumped 28 percent between 2004 and 2009.[3] The survey describes the fallout for these caregivers: 16 percent report a toll on their health, 31 percent describe high emotional stress, and nearly two-thirds of those with jobs say they go to work late, leave early, or take time off during the day to care for their parents and older relatives.[4]

Despite the emotional, social, and financial costs, we soldier on unarmed against trouble. We fend for ourselves and hope things work out. The result? Too many crises, too few full-fledged crisis survivors, and an expanding population of walking wounded on the professional and personal fronts alike.

The Way Forward

This book offers a positive alternative for companies and their employees. Use it like a road map that will show you how to avoid becoming crisis "roadkill" on life's highway. Learn how to stand up, avert most disasters, and resolve other crises that come your way. If you're a supervisor or manager, equip yourself with strategies to mentor struggling coworkers. The mission: turn pain into profit by empowering employees to be more engaged and more productive.

Major companies and their executives have called on me to help them overcome their business crises triggered by hostile takeovers, class action lawsuits, criminal prosecutions, and congressional hearings. Companies routinely prevent crises by auditing their businesses and fixing problems before they become major-league messes. When crises do occur, a company's crisis management team ideally does the following:

- They review their crisis management plan and talk through the company's business, communications, and legal goals.

- They identify the risks and opportunities the crisis presents and analyze the options to consider, the people and resources to deploy, and the allies and experts to call upon.

- They debate, argue, and finally agree on a strategy to implement.

- They stay in constant contact to gauge how they're doing and make adjustments as the crisis unfolds.

- They look for how to be stronger *after* the crisis abates.

These techniques, implemented by America's top companies, are the keys to corporate crisis management. Since companies are ultimately people, too, why not absorb the best of how they respond to their crises? I adapted corporate techniques into a four-step *"Instant Survivor™* System" to deal with crises in my life and in the lives of my clients, family, and friends. You can use these steps to prevent trouble in your life and for those you care about. This system is not foolproof, but it is the best way for you to become an *Instant Survivor™*.

The Instant Survivor™ System

Here are the four steps of my *Instant Survivor™* System that will enable you to conquer professional and personal crises.

STAY FROSTY: Keep your emotions in check as you develop a crisis management plan. As you maintain this frosty perspective, you must be selfish by focusing first on yourself, then on the facts of the situation.

SECURE SUPPORT: Call on friends, family, and advisors. Build your personal crisis management team that will root for you and help you implement your plan, move fast to respond to trouble, and stay visible to your allies.

STAND TALL: Control the crisis, not vice versa. Modify your action plan in writing, take personal responsibility, make sound early decisions, stay flexible while pursuing a solution, and send simple, positive messages to your community about your crisis response.

SAVE YOUR FUTURE: Act to prevent crises. Take an audit of yourself and the key parts of your life, detect trouble areas and bolster weaknesses, and train yourself to respond well to upheavals.

By following this four-step *Instant Survivor*™ System—stay frosty, secure support, stand tall, and save your future—you will be alert to pending trouble, you will remain focused, you will be rational when a crisis strikes, and you will soon put it behind you.

My Own Experience

The crucible for this book is my own life. At age forty, I lost a race for statewide political office and felt like a leper: alone, ignored, no job prospects, savings nil. At best, I figured I was a mere footnote in Maryland political history. Thankfully, friends rescued me from the deep end of the pool and offered me work.

Six years later I left my law firm to become the general counsel of a white-hot fiber optics company. Lifelong political aspirations spawned this risky calculation. In my vision, God would reach down and rejuvenate my dream: the company would shoot up like a rocket, go public, turn paper stock options into gold, bankroll a winning campaign, and help transform Maryland government. In reality, my wife agreed to the job's steep pay cut and we took a big gamble on the company's success.

Do you remember how the dot-com craze morphed into the dot-com crater? My fiber optics company was not immune. Stock options worth pennies shredded my plans for a self-funded campaign. With two children headed toward college, another career misstep or misfire in the economy would completely ruin us. But even though my long-lived political dream had died, my challenges were just beginning.

My crisis was not a "hard" one such as storm damage to a dwelling. It was what you might call a "soft" crisis—often the most challenging type in life. Crises that fall in this category include an "identity crisis," a "crisis of confidence," or a "spiritual crisis." My particular crisis was all three wrapped in one.

Questions hammered my brain. Who am I? What can I do? How should I fill up my life? How could I help others? How can I keep my head high? Where will I find resources to muster enthusiasm for work and life amid grief over my shattered dream?

My previous work with companies to help them resolve their catastrophes led me out of my desperation toward my personal four-step rescue plan. If corporations implement a strategy that works, why shouldn't I? More to the point of this book, why shouldn't *you*?

To move past political failure and recharge the sense of meaning in my life, I followed the four steps of my *Instant Survivor*™ System. To keep my emotions in check, I drafted a plan to explore new life paths. I secured support from others. A "life coach" advised building on my success handling crises for companies. A Texas sports psychologist who helps NBA teams and PGA golfers win championships walked and played golf and talked with me. He introduced what was to me a new concept: do not define yourself by past success or failure. We explored the idea of preparation. We contemplated faith. During this "identity-confidence-spiritual" crisis, I tried to stand tall as a steady husband and father. My mantra was to give my family lots of time, stay physically fit, and succeed at work.

When offered the opportunity to share my expertise with others, I saved my future. Now my work includes my love—helping managers and company employees prevent, prepare for, and fix their personal and professional crises, serving as their advisor, speaker, and consultant. Having succeeded in helping Fortune 500 companies and individuals overcome crises, I wanted to bring my four-step system to a broader audience.

That's why I wrote *The Instant Survivor*. You hold the book I could not find when I went to the bookstore after trouble struck.

Learn from my stories of victorious, high-profile professionals and other crisis survivors. Read on to master the crisis management techniques and tools of top companies. Stop being overwhelmed by your personal and professional crises. Start using this four-step system so you and your people can become Instant Survivors.

STAY FROSTY

We are routinely told to "stay calm" when we face a crisis. But how are we supposed to do that?

Step One supplies the program by giving you the tools to stay objective about your situation and take action. Staying frosty means calmly moving forward while freezing out negative emotions of fear, anger, and bitterness.

Chapter one helps you create your own crisis management plan. Companies rely on them to stop the panic, develop a strategy, and get into gear. Remember how poor Chicken Little ran around proclaiming that the sky was falling? Isn't that how we react when the roof caves in on our lives? With a plan in place, you will respond quickly and intelligently when trouble hits.

Chapter two encourages you to embrace your selfishness. Yes. To survive a crisis, you need to be self-focused on your recovery.

Chapter three illuminates how to gather other facts about what's wrong. Do so deliberately and unemotionally—the way a detective pursues a case.

By creating a crisis management plan, learning to be selfish, and gathering facts about your situation, you will stay frosty.

1

EMERGENCY ROOM PROTOCOL

Believe it or not, creating a written plan can help you survive and thrive. Companies rely on written crisis management plans, not because they lay out a cookbook solution to every crisis, but because the best ones pose a series of questions that unlock frozen brains and guide them toward a solution. A written crisis management plan will work for you, too. In order to use a crisis management plan, however, you have to remain cool, calm, and collected—just as Isabel Gillies managed to do as she faced the most daunting crisis of her life.

"Is this really happening?"

Fall in rural Ohio is deceptively peaceful. The trees envelop you in a soft tableau of colors. The quiet, remote setting suggests safety and security. The well-known college where you and your husband teach magnifies the cozy feeling.

Isabel Gillies had moved to Ohio so her husband could follow his dream of being a professor. She gave up her dream of being an actress and took a teaching job instead. They had two young boys.

She spent her days taking care of them, teaching, and enjoying meals and college activities with other faculty members.

When a new female professor joined her husband's department, Isabel befriended her. A month later, Isabel's husband left her and their sons for this new friend.[1]

You may know Isabel Gillies. Her acting roles include Detective Stabler's wife on the TV show *Law and Order: Special Victims Unit*. When I met Isabel, she told me her husband's betrayal made her ask herself repeatedly, "Is this really happening?" Life suddenly looked bleak for her. She was heartbroken, desperate for money, and seemingly sentenced to a solo life of struggle. How would she stay frosty after a burning earthquake struck her life?

Fortunately for Gillies, her "plan B" thinking kicked in. She immediately outlined what she should do, acting just like a member of a corporate crisis management team. "You sort of start thinking about [plan B] right away and I think it's baloney if people say you don't . . . I really think we're survivalist people."

Her thinking evolved quickly: "If it's really happening, a series of things is going to happen. I'm going to have to find my children new schools to go to. I'm going to have to call people in the town I'm going to move back to, to make sure I'm going to have a job or a babysitter. I'm going to have to find love again. How is that going to happen?"

In her book *Happens Every Day*, Isabel says about plan Bs: "They are hard to swallow, but they are better than nothing and they *are* a plan. . . . Having a plan, even if it's a meager plan, is useful and gets you through."[2]

Isabel said her best determination during her crisis was that how she handled it wasn't really about her, but about her children. "How am I going to see this man as my children's father, really? It was so clear how much they loved him and love him, and I don't really have that much room to dislike this man. I have to incorporate him into my life in another way, almost like I have to translate him into another language. . . . You have to make it not too bad for your kids. It's not their fault."

Focus on a New Future

While Isabel focused on a new future, she simultaneously faced a gyrating wave of feelings. She found herself crying, not just privately in the shower but openly in public, in the copy shop. But the sadness did not stop her from moving forward. "Sadness is soft, and I can live with sadness. I could just be sad all day and get a lot done." Her anger, however, constrained her like a suit of hard plastic. "It doesn't move, and you can't do other things while you're angry . . . you're cut off. . . . I think if you're really angry, you have to go and get help. I don't know if you can deal with it yourself."

Isabel felt a tremendous sense of failure—that she had failed at her marriage—particularly since her husband must have found it so unbearable to live with her that he wanted to leave their children.

She also carried a heavy sense of shame. "You just want to be the norm. . . . My husband left me right around Christmastime, and all of the Christmas cards were coming to our family. Happy families in front; happy families all together. And I was like, oh my God, am I such a loser? I don't have that. I just lost it in front of my kids. There is a sense of shame."

Isabel found that the solving of her crisis is what got her through it. "It's like if someone takes away your ball on the playground. Are you going to just sit there and not have a ball or are you going to go find another one, or figure out how to get that one back? . . . I don't want to just suddenly be in my nightgown all the time, drinking."

She and her husband went to see a counselor to try and save their marriage, but the effort was fruitless; her husband had moved on. Isabel gave up trying to get her husband back. She and her children moved back to live with her parents in New York City. She didn't want to do this. "I did not want to live with my parents and my children, and they didn't want to live with me." But it worked out. Isabel got her kids into schools midyear (no easy deal in New York City), wrote a best-selling book about the collapse of her marriage, and resumed a successful acting career. She also got remarried and has managed to make friends with her ex-husband and his new wife.

Isabel managed not just to survive but to thrive in the wake of a serious life crisis. That's the goal we have for ourselves: stay frosty; move through, past, and beyond our troubles; and step into bright, warm sunshine.

Unlock Your Frozen Brain

We risk freezing in place when trouble comes. It scares us, befuddles us, and depresses us. When I asked in an online survey what people first thought when things went wrong in their lives, three responses were the big winners: "Oh sh**," "Oh fu**," and "Oh my God." You probably have those same responses, but we all know they don't exactly produce careful analysis and quick action.

Companies understand that moving fast can mean the difference between life and death. A poignant example is this discovery: the National Institute of Standards and Technology conducted a post-9/11 investigation and determined that about one thousand employees in the Twin Towers took the time to shut down their computers after the airplanes hit.[3] Even nonfatal situations can't afford needless delay.

Fast action in the face of disaster is likely to produce a better outcome, and a speedy response is far more likely when you have a plan in place. Let's look at the exact sections your crisis management plan should contain by drafting one right now.

Instant Survivor™ Alert

We will develop a written plan you can pull out at the first warning sign of trouble and use to determine what's wrong and what to do about it. (*The Instant Survivor*™ Handbook, which you can download for free at www.instantsurvivor.com, contains a crisis management plan template for you.) Your plan should have three sections: Diagnosis, Action, and After-Action Report. If you want to modify these sections or add new ones, go ahead. The plan is meant to work for you.

MANAGER TIP #1—EMERGENCY ROOM PROTOCOL

If you have a colleague who is suffering a personal or professional crisis, ask him or her this question:

What are you thinking about as a potential plan B?

Diagnosis

You can diagnose your problem by answering a series of questions. Of course, sometimes the crisis is obvious: you suffer a debilitating injury from a car crash, your house is destroyed by a tornado, your father is diagnosed with Alzheimer's. But often several issues are jumbled together or mask other problems. For example, a car crash could stem from undiagnosed alcoholism. A marriage could be faltering because a spouse lost a job and the couple now faces financial problems. Crises don't obey boundaries. Even when the problem is obvious, there's value in writing it down because it focuses you on facts rather than emotions. Try to follow a 20/80 approach: spend 20 percent of your time analyzing the problem and 80 percent figuring out and producing a solution. This helps you move from "Why is this happening to me?" to "How can I move forward?"

A good way to diagnose what is wrong is to write down the answers to the following questions. To demonstrate the process, we'll look back at Isabel's situation and see how she might have answered them.

1. What is your problem?

Your problem is what you "own," what you can control. Define it carefully. Don't try to fix what isn't yours because you don't control it. If there are several problems, divide a page in thirds or quarters and address each one separately.

Isabel: My husband is leaving me for another woman. This means I need to rebuild the lives of myself and my children.

2. What are your goals in the situation?

Focus on the complete menu of goals. For example, if you have lost your job, your short-term goal might be to reduce your expenses and generate quick revenue (perhaps via a yard sale or eBay) since you don't know how long you'll be out of work. A medium-term goal might be to find a replacement job, which could be part-time work or a full-time job outside your current field or lower-paying work in your field, as a stopgap measure. Finding well-paying, satisfying full-time work might be your long-term goal.

Isabel: My short-term goal is to find a new place to live and schools for my children. My medium-term goals are to find paid work I like and to fall in love again. My most important long-term goal is to protect my children so they can lead normal lives and not be caught in the crossfire between my ex-husband and me.

3. How did the problem come to your attention?

Many crises are slow burning and gather heat over time. If so, looking back may help you focus on the nature of the problem and its solution.

Isabel: My husband told me our marriage was over. When I look back, I see numerous warning signs that should have told me he was a high-risk husband and that he was having an affair. I will keep this in mind when and if I think about getting married again.

4. How are you feeling about this situation?

Don't ignore your feelings. Pour them out. Talk about what you're worried about, angry about, bitter about. It will help you move from victim to survivor.

Isabel: I feel stupid, angry at my husband and his girlfriend, sad, ashamed, and like I'm a failure.

5. What facts do you know right now?

Making a solid diagnosis requires examining the facts in a clinical manner. Pretend you're looking down from a balcony on the scene below and can see yourself. Take an unemotional view. This is an essential step to staying frosty.

Isabel: I know that my marriage is in trouble since my husband is having an affair.

6. What other information do you need to find out?

What else do you need to know to decide on the best action steps to take?

Isabel: I want to see if I can save my marriage before I give up on it and move on. I need to figure out where my children and I can live and where I can work if my marriage is over.

7. Who can I call on for help?

Who are the friends, relatives, professionals, or support groups I can ask for assistance?

Isabel: I can call my parents and see if they will offer to take us in.

8. How can the crisis get worse?

Make sure you understand the full dimensions of the problem before trying to solve it.

Isabel: I will be in trouble financially and emotionally if my parents won't let us live with them. In case they won't or it doesn't work out, I will examine other short-term options for staying with friends while I identify work I can pick up immediately to pay rent for a place to live for the longer term.

9. What is the cure for the crisis?

Follow the 20/80 rule. Spend 20 percent of your time on the problem and 80 percent of your time on the solution.

Isabel: Move back in with my parents, find schools that will accept my kids midyear, and find work.

Action

After diagnosing the problem, the next challenge is to decide what to do. Here are questions to ask to help you outline direct and immediate actions to take.

1. What steps can I take . . .

To contain the damage from the crisis?

To address the immediate symptoms?

To solve the crisis for the long term?

Isabel: Arrange a meeting with a marriage counselor to see if my marriage can be saved. If my marriage is over, call my parents and friends, contact schools, and stay open to life and love once I've moved.

2. What are the concrete tasks to perform? Who will do them? What is the deadline for their completion?

Isabel: Contact a marriage counselor immediately, then make a list of the people and schools I need to contact if I'm going to move.

After-Action Report

Once the crisis is over, you should look back to assess how you performed under pressure. What did you do well and how can you improve next time? This is the critical third stage of a crisis management plan, yet many people are tempted to skip it. Step Four of my system, "Save Your Future," is devoted to this important process of self-examination and provides concrete ways to improve each area of your life.

Let's see how Isabel might look back and examine how she handled her marriage crisis.

> **EMERGENCY ROOM PROTOCOL**
>
> - Stay frosty as you consider any crisis.
> - Develop a crisis management plan with three stages.
>   - Diagnosis (What's the problem?)
>   - Action (What can I do?)
>   - After-Action Report (What did I do well and what could I improve?)

Isabel: I ignored warning signs about my husband's faithfulness and commitment and the danger presented by this newly arrived "friend." My antennae are now up for threats to my relationships. Once I knew that my marriage was over, I responded well by moving back to New York City, protecting my children, and building a new life. Now that I'm remarried, I work hard not to repeat mistakes from my first marriage.

You're Not Good to Go

So, you've written a plan that will help you manage any crisis. It might seem like you're good to go. Hold on a minute. This is just the first step to becoming an *Instant Survivor*™.

Think back on the giant companies that thought they were ready, had crisis management plans and experienced crisis teams in place, and then totally botched a crisis: Bear Stearns, Enron, and Lehman Brothers, to name but a few. Think about the big shots who mangled the personal disasters they faced: Dick Cheney, Tiger Woods, and Bill Clinton. They all had high-powered advisors, yet each one flunked when a crisis struck.

•   •   •

In crisis management, as in professional sports, the game looks easier from the stands. Handling a crisis well is not a paint-by-number operation. If a plug-and-play approach existed for crisis management, then the landscape wouldn't be littered with large and small companies and famous and everyday people who crashed and burned when thrust into the pilot's hot seat.

But believe me, you can do this, especially if you accept that you'll need to focus exclusively on yourself when a crisis hits.

NUMBER ONE IS JOB ONE

When a crisis hits, management often wonders where to focus its efforts: On the consumers who may have been injured by the crisis? On the employees? On the shareholders?

I encourage my corporate clients to focus on protecting their reputations and on the survival of their companies. By overcoming the crisis and prospering in the future, the company will be best positioned to serve customers, employees, and shareholders. As strange as it may seem, being selfish allows a company to act in the most unselfish manner.

You may be turned off by my recommendation that you also be selfish during a crisis. We are taught at an early age that being selfish is wrong. Yet there is a running debate in intellectual circles about whether selfishness is required for individuals to become great entrepreneurs, scientists, and other achievers. You'll want to embrace it as a crucial second step to staying frosty. Let's examine the story of one woman who chose to live for herself and, in so doing, became an *Instant Survivor™*.

A Rough Diagnosis

Robin Roberts, anchor of ABC's *Good Morning America,* has been an athlete all her life and dreamed of playing pro basketball. She watches what she eats. She doesn't drink to excess and doesn't smoke. She's very active. Discipline and self-control brought her success as a college basketball player and as a broadcaster.

So, when she was diagnosed with breast cancer in July 2007, Robin was angry. As she exclaimed to me in a recent conversation, "Hey, wait a minute, I've done the things that you're supposed to do!" She felt scared and embarrassed. She worried other people might think she had done something wrong, since she got cancer despite always preaching about the need to take care of one's health. No longer was she just "Robin" but "Robin with breast cancer."[1] As a result, she felt out of control. She told me, "That was the hardest thing, to know that I was not in control."

Her doctor explained to her that her lifestyle was not going to prevent her from getting cancer, "But, boy, it's really going to help you kick it in the butt." Robin described her response: "Once I looked at it that way . . . my disappointment waned a little bit and I got excited because it was like this big opponent, and I love opponents. And I said—Okay, okay, you got the upper hand, you got the lead in the first quarter, but I can come back and win this thing. That's how I approached it, and it really helped."

Robin was determined to put herself, not cancer, in control of her life. That is how she managed to stay frosty. Several days before her surgery she decided to announce on *Good Morning America* that she had cancer. "Cancer is very personal, and when you're going through any type of crisis, the last thing you feel like doing is sharing." Her mother told her that she could be a voice for others facing cancer, and Robin decided that there was a purpose beyond her disease. "Many times when you're going through a crisis, you feel like a victim. When I was able to gather the strength to go public, I was the one who was really benefiting in the end. That was the first night I slept like a baby, right after I had announced, because I felt prayers being said, I felt the good wishes, I felt like now I was sharing the burden. I wasn't having to face it all on my own."

"You live life for yourself."

After her partial mastectomy and lymph node surgery, Robin was sore. Then it was time to start chemotherapy, to be followed by radiation treatments. Many friends told her not to rush returning to work. But Robin lives by the philosophy that "you live life for yourself." She craved a normal life. She also remembered that when anchor Peter Jennings announced he had throat cancer, he said he planned to be back on the air but never was able to do so. Robin thought, "I have got to get back, I just do; if not for myself, for our viewers, for my colleagues. I don't want them to be thinking, 'Oh boy, here we go again.'" Ten days after her surgery, Robin was back at work.

At first, Robin looked normal after her surgery, but then she began to lose her hair. "I was doing really fine . . . until I lost my hair—that's what was so traumatic. Then it was like, oh my gosh, now I look like someone who has cancer. Now I can't hide it anymore."

She decided to shave off her hair. She went to a hairdresser who shaved it all off. "I remember I didn't cry. I just looked in the mirror and was like, aha, taking control again! I got control over you now, cancer! I decided that this was the day I was going to lose my hair. You didn't decide it."

"I Double-Dog Dare You"

During her cancer treatment, she and her colleagues came up with the idea of confronting each other with the game "I Double-Dog Dare You." Her coworkers challenged Robin to be in a New York City fashion show. Twenty professional models walked before her down the runway. Just before she turned the corner to step out in her red sequined dress, Robin saw a mirror and decided to take off her "little trusty anchor hair wig," which she had been wearing to avoid scaring viewers. She said to herself: "No, take the wig off, just take it off. This is about being comfortable with who you are, where you are." She held her head high and beamed, thinking "This is me. Take me as I am." As she explains, "It was a very meaningful moment for me." Her bald-headed walk on the catwalk inspired many and left some in tears.

Robin's philosophy—to live life for herself—is a valuable crisis creed. Robin knew that to conquer her cancer she had to be "selfish," which meant upholding her values and approach to life as opposed to what others might choose for her. During a crisis we are vulnerable to losing track of ourselves and our identities and to submitting easily to the ideas and suggestions of others, which may not be right for us.

Robin conquered cancer by keeping control and by staying true to herself. She identified cancer as an opponent she could beat. She made crucial decisions along the way to demonstrate her control: to go public, to go back to work during treatment, to shave off her hair, and to remove her wig. Her decisions attracted support, new friends, and prayers.

Yet she also understood that to survive a crisis, it helps to know why you want to get past it, which may involve other people. I asked Robin, "When you got diagnosed, what were you fighting for?" Robin paused and said, "I was really fighting for my mom . . . I had always heard how devastating it was for a parent to bury a child . . . I just could not put the burden on her, my siblings, my family, or my friends."

She also told me, "Let me tell you right now, I am so proud of being a survivor."

Crisis survivors endure because they are self-focused—they know who they are, they understand why survival is important to them, they figure out what they need to do to move past the crisis, and they do it. This mind-set allows us to stay frosty no matter what trouble crops up.

Instant Survivor™ Alert

Forget the pointy-headed debates and what you learned in kindergarten. The point here is basic. When companies are in trouble, they need single-minded focus to get out of it. They have to be selfish and act in their own self-interest.

MANAGER TIP #2—NUMBER ONE IS JOB ONE

If you have a colleague who is suffering a personal or professional crisis, ask him or her this question:

Why is it important to you to get past this issue?

If we don't act selfishly in a crisis, we prolong our problems, and the result is that we lose and the people who depend on us lose as well. A crisis gives you a free pass to be selfish (or self-focused, if that word choice makes you feel better). Take advantage of it. Be strong in your selfishness because it will make your crisis shorter. You will resume your regular life faster and reassure your friends, family, and others that you are in control. By doing what's best for you, you are acting in the best interests of those who depend on you. Take off your superwoman or superman cape, skip trying to do everything, acknowledge what's wrong, and spend the time and energy to fix it.

•   •   •

NUMBER ONE IS JOB ONE

- Take control of your crisis so it doesn't control you.

- Live through and survive the crisis on your terms.

- Focus on yourself and your needs—it will help you survive.

- Figure out why it's important to you to overcome this challenge.

Maybe you think that a single-minded, selfish focus is essential only when you're sick and trying to recover, like Robin Roberts did. But whatever the disaster—divorce, debt, death of a loved one, dismissal from a job—your devoted attention is required to stay frosty and move on to getting the facts.

JUST THE FACTS, MA'AM

Whenever I work with a corporate client facing a crisis, I focus on the facts, *Dragnet* style. I sit down with the senior executives and analyze the crisis, piece by excruciating piece. Who exactly is involved? What caused the crisis? What do we know so far and what do we need to find out? What is the company's financial exposure? How can the crisis get worse? What has the company done to protect consumers, shareholders, suppliers, and employees? How will we define successful handling of the crisis? What are they doing to make sure it won't happen again? I then review all the relevant documents, internal company communications, press releases, and memos and go back to the client with more questions. Without complete transparency, without a focus on the facts, a crisis can spin out of control.

The third component to staying frosty is to maintain your focus on the facts. This task is a lot easier to say than do, however. Under stress we often forget the importance of facts and instead let our emotions take over. We feel sorry for ourselves, kick ourselves, or blame others for our predicament, and we daydream about when life will return to normal. We are afraid of what might happen; we fear the great unknown. When we let our emotions dominate as we face a mess, we fail to connect dots that should be connected. Instead, we end up linking dots that are best left alone or separate. Meanwhile, what happens when our emotions swing wildly? One moment we have our problem in hand; the next moment, we are helpless, our situation hopeless. We run "hot" instead of staying frosty.

How do we escape this emotional vice? Gather facts with a purpose and a clinical approach. In a crisis, two goals are paramount: *pin down what is wrong* and *identify a solution to solve it*. While some crises resist an immediate fix, there are always ways to improve our situation, provided we understand and acknowledge the problems we face.

Let's examine the challenges involved in gathering and interpreting facts by meeting a media star who faced a severe career threat.

"It's all in your head."

Diane Rehm is a National Public Radio talk show host with two million listeners who eagerly anticipate hearing her voice on a daily basis. About twenty years ago, she developed a shallow cough. At the time, she had been taking Advil to help her sleep and deal with headaches and other body complaints. Soon the cough started to interfere with her on-air interviews because she would cough in the middle of a sentence. After her doctor checked her out and specialists stuck tubes down her throat, she was told that there was nothing wrong. She then happened to notice a warning on the Advil bottle stating that the painkiller can produce asthma-like symptoms, which include a cough.[1]

The experts had failed her. In the end, Diane diagnosed herself and cured her cough. But new voice problems cropped up. A raspy hoarseness set in several times a year, and then her voice began to quiver. When her producer asked her about it, Diane waved her off and waited a year before consulting a throat specialist, even though her quiver had gotten steadily worse. Another succession of doctors examined her, putting more tubes down her throat, and told her: "It's all in your head."

Diane noticed that the quiver made her nervous, and the more nervous she got, the more the tremor occurred. Diane had not graduated from high school, and for years she had fought low self-esteem. She decided that her voice problems were triggered by her brain's recognition that she was inadequate. She repeatedly told herself, "You have no place here, you don't deserve to be here." She was afraid, partially due to her "impostor complex." Her program had recently gone national. The doctors recommended various medications, including Prilosec (to stop acid reflux) and Inderal (a beta blocker used to lower blood pressure). Neither medication worked. A top-notch speech pathologist worked with Diane on breath support, which helped slightly but didn't cure the unreliability of her voice.[2]

Diane began researching her voice problem. She learned her symptoms matched spasmodic dysphonia, a rare, incurable but nevertheless treatable voice disorder. She asked her voice coach and the doctors whether it was possible that she had spasmodic dysphonia. They all but convinced her that her problems were in her head. Her voice worsened. It quivered, cracked, croaked, and occasionally didn't work at all. It was at that point, she told me during our interview, that she "was scared that somebody was going to come to me and say, 'You cannot be on the air anymore.'"

Diane avoided talking to her employer. The show was growing by leaps and bounds and she was afraid that talking about the problem would open the door to her departure. Finally she gave in after suffering a panic attack during a conference where she was a panelist. She took an indefinite leave of absence, went home, and sat alone, quietly. She began three months of visits to pharmacological, cognitive behavioral, and speech therapists.[3] She felt better about herself, but her voice didn't get any better.

Ready to Quit

Diane told me she was ready after that three-month leave of absence to quit, to give up her career. Her doctor then sent her off to Johns Hopkins University in Baltimore to be examined by yet another group of specialists. The first one assured her that she didn't have Parkinson's or ALS (Lou Gehrig's disease). The next one reviewed the results of prior tests and concluded immediately that she had spasmodic dysphonia. Diane's reaction: "I thought so."

Diane had a choice to make in order to address the symptoms of spasmodic dysphonia: take an anticonvulsant called Mysoline, which might take as long as four to six weeks to work, or inject Botox (which paralyzes muscles) into her vocal chords. Her husband rejected the Botox approach, but Diane had read about it and its effects and peppered the doctor with a series of questions. "Could it make my voice worse? Does regular use hurt the vocal chords? If I stop taking the Botox shots will my voice be worse than it was before?"[4] The answer to all three questions was no. Diane decided she wanted to try the Botox. That day the doctor injected her vocal chords with Botox, and within three weeks Diane was back on the air, where she has remained for more than ten years. Her radio show, *The Diane Rehm Show*, keeps gaining new stations and listeners.

Diane has been an advocate for spasmodic dysphonia sufferers, serving as an honorary member on the Spasmodic Dysphonia Association board and hosting a program on her show about her voice problems and the disease. Also, she has moved past her feelings that she is an impostor. When she was asked to give a speech and discovered there was no podium, the event manager assured her she'd be fine without it. "I got up there, free as a bird, and just started talking and had people laughing and cheering. I think that was when I first began to shed that impostor feeling, and now I don't feel it."

Connecting Unconnected Dots

Diane's struggle underscores how hard it is to stay frosty and gather facts successfully in the midst of a crisis. She trumped the doctors by recognizing that the source of her cough was Advil. She connected dots they had missed. She then mistakenly connected dots by concluding that her voice quiver was her body's cry of recognition that she did not belong in the high-profile job she held. She first tried to ignore her voice problems, only seeing a specialist when her quiver became too intense. She finally took a leave of absence when her voice, along with her self-confidence, had virtually disappeared.

Most important, though, Diane persisted throughout her eight-year struggle. She felt sure her problems weren't just in her head; as a result, she did her own research. She consulted the *Physicians' Desk Reference* and learned about the symptoms of spasmodic dysphonia. Before she was even diagnosed with it, she knew about the treatment alternatives and the benefits of Botox. She endured a succession of disheartening and incorrect diagnoses by ten doctors before being accurately diagnosed. She also worked on addressing the source of her low self-esteem—a highly critical mother—facing squarely the skeletons in her family closet. As a result, Diane saved her career and herself.

How to Get the Facts

What can we learn from Diane and others about how to stay frosty and gather facts in the face of disaster?

PRACTICE EXTREME HONESTY. We need to be as honest with ourselves as we demand others to be with us. How do we like to be treated when things go sour—when we get laid off, hear bad health news, or have a relationship broken off? We want to be told the truth. We reject people who shade a story: "They're feeding us a bunch of BS"; "He's sending sunshine up my a___"; "They're treating us like mushrooms—keeping us in the dark and feeding us sh**."

But we cut ourselves slack when we talk to ourselves about trouble in our lives. We downplay it, dismiss it, deny it. Make-believe is a fun game to play as a kid but can be life-threatening for adults. So when we face trouble, we should demand from ourselves the same truth—both good and bad—that we demand from others.

About ten years ago, the Department of Veterans Affairs got tired of getting sued so often by unhappy ex-soldiers. Consequently, it pursued an "extreme honesty policy," which involved keeping each patient informed regularly and aggressively, no matter what happened, but especially when mistakes and errors occurred. The result: fewer lawsuits.[5] Be extremely honest with yourself. We all make mistakes; just admit it, fix it, and move on.

When the world-famous influenza epidemic of 1918 gripped Britain, public officials in a few British cities informed citizens about what precautions to take, told the truth about the dangers, and gave them ideas on how to cope. While national fatalities ranked in the tens of thousands, many deaths were prevented in these cities. In his essay "Pandemics: Avoiding the Mistakes of 1918," John M. Barry concluded, "Where people had accurate information and knew what they faced, they often performed heroically."[6] Tell yourself the truth and you will respond intelligently and courageously.

CHECK YOUR EMOTIONS. Ah, my friend, we can gain wisdom from poker players too. Amy Duke is a poker professional, frequently winning Texas Hold'em tournaments. Listen to her analysis: "Poker teaches you that there are things you have control over and things that you don't. When you have a bad outcome, you analyze the decision chain and try to figure out if it was a decision that went wrong. If it's out of your control, the deal of the deck, don't get 'tilted,' which means emotionally upset. That's unproductive and will make things fall apart in the future. We all make very poor decisions when we're out of emotional control."[7]

Beware of a prime enemy of careful fact-gathering: uncontrolled emotion. A recent study concluded that many Americans defaulted on their homes recently out of anger, fear, or despair instead of making sensible decisions about what was best for them financially.[8]

FACE BAD FACTS BRAVELY. Scientists recently discovered a gene mutation that predisposes women to develop breast and ovarian cancer. According to the American Cancer Society, women with the BRCA gene mutations are 60 to 80 percent more likely to develop breast cancer, which is five times higher than the general population, and face up to a 60 percent chance of getting ovarian cancer. Many women have chosen to be tested for the gene. Meredith Grossfield told CNN, "I keep telling myself that it's better to know and be ready."[9] Some women have bought life insurance policies in advance of their genetic tests. Others, knowing that cancer could force removal of their ovaries, have frozen their eggs to allow for later pregnancies. Some have chosen to get double mastectomies to prevent the risk of developing breast cancer. They have faced bad facts and taken courageous action to overcome a personal crisis.

RELY ON HUMOR. When I visited wounded soldiers at Walter Reed Army Medical Center, a major rehabilitation center near Washington, DC, for injured troops, I witnessed their no-nonsense, fact-focused, no-pity approach to their injuries. In a workout room, soldiers with missing eyes and limbs pressed weights, stretched out, and trash-talked each other. They told me matter-of-factly about their wounds, their treatment, and their recovery prospects. One described how an EFP (explosively formed projectile) had blown through the floor of his Humvee, killed the soldier seated next to him, and sheared off his own leg. They also rely on humor. "What's an amputee's favorite restaurant?" Staff Sergeant Brian Schar, who lost both legs in Iraq, asked a *Washington Post* reporter. "IHOP."[10] Americans chuckled when President Ronald Reagan reported telling his wife after the assassination attempt by John Hinckley Jr., "Honey, I forgot to duck!" Being able to laugh at ourselves reduces pressure, gives us a healthy perspective on a crisis, and enables us to maintain the emotional distance we need to gather facts and take appropriate action.

BE PATIENT AND PERSISTENT. Sometimes solutions take time, or something you try really isn't a solution at all. This doesn't mean that you haven't survived a crisis. By working to find the facts of what went wrong and how your situation can be improved, you immediately become a survivor—working thoughtfully and unemotionally in your best interests. You could call this a victory in itself.

Instant Survivor™ Alert

To gain perspective on your own life problems, you might need some tricks to help you clear the lenses through which you're viewing your circumstances. Pretend you're a hired detective; keep your emotional distance from the situation. Or consider yourself a journalist hired to (a) write a story about your struggle and (b) find a solution to your crisis. Part of your role as a journalist requires talking to others—friends, family members, experts—about how to approach the situation and what to do about it. Or picture yourself on a balcony looking down on the situation: this will give you a perspective on your troubles that promotes clear analysis and assessment. Remember how Isabel Gillies had to take that aerial, unemotional view when her husband deserted her?

MANAGER TIP #3—JUST THE FACTS, MA'AM

If you have a colleague who is suffering a personal or professional crisis, ask him or her this question:

What do you need to find out to improve your understanding of the situation?

While you're clearing your head and improving your point of view, be wary of your natural instinct to find the quick fix of the so-called experts. Because we're often so desperate to improve our situation, we latch onto an expert's view and treat it as God-given. Keep your own wits about you, along with a healthy dose of skepticism. While commonly accepted experts can give useful advice, crises often defy an easy diagnosis, and experts can be wrong.

Finally, gather facts about yourself. Who are you and how do you tend to react when trouble erupts? If you're typically calm, then maintain that approach despite the pressure. If you're wired for sound and easily agitated, "stay frosty" so you can analyze what's wrong and how to cure it.

· · ·

Remember, in order to stay frosty as you face a personal crisis, you must be sure to get as much information as possible about the situation and adopt the right attitude.

When a crisis hits, top companies react with composure. Others flub by taking challenges personally and worsen the situation by responding emotionally. You, too, will be tempted to do this. Don't. Instead of rushing to take action, copy what sharp companies do: review your crisis management plan, focus on yourself, and gather as many facts as possible. Only then will you be able to stay frosty and take the next step on the path to becoming an *Instant Survivor*™: secure support.

JUST THE FACTS, MA'AM

- Practice extreme honesty.
- Check your emotions.
- Face bad facts bravely.
- Rely on humor.
- Be patient and persistent.

SECURE SUPPORT

The U.S. Marines teach their warriors that they should do everything in pairs. The mandate is built on the premise that a solo Marine is easy to kill whereas two Marines are hard as hell to kill.[1] Step Two addresses why it is essential to secure support during a crisis and how to do it. In chapters four through seven, you will see that you should seek support from relatives, friends, and support groups. They will prop you up, guide you, encourage you, and give you perspective. Two definitions of the word "secure" apply in this discussion. The first meaning is to acquire, or get possession of, support. Chapter four describes how to ask others for help, how support groups can bolster you in your struggle, and how to build your own crisis management team. The second meaning of "secure" is to make firm or tight. Chapters five through seven will show you how to tighten the support you will gain. Chapter five advises responding quickly when trouble arrives, while chapter six highlights the importance of staying visible during a disaster. Chapter seven underscores why we must apologize quickly and fully when we make a mistake in order to firm up the support of our friends and allies.

ONE IS THE
LONELIEST NUMBER

"Americans like the cowboy who leads the wagon train by riding ahead on his horse, the cowboy who rides all alone into the town, the village, with his horse and nothing else,"[1] said former Secretary of State Henry Kissinger. Companies today understand the marketing appeal of the lone cowboy. Philip Morris, the cigarette company, enshrined the romantic notion of the loner cowboy with its invention of the Marlboro Man—a rugged macho man shown brandishing his iconic smoke. Sales skyrocketed.

But companies realize that when it comes to dealing with a crisis, the cavalry is much more effective than one lone cowboy. When a company runs into a crisis, the first thing they do is call upon their crisis management *team*. One manager would never take it upon him- or herself to attempt to solve the company's major problem. A manager may take over as a leader, but that individual relies on experts to support all aspects of the organization's business. The crisis team will include representatives from the finance, operations, human relations, public relations, and legal departments—and others as needed. The company will also secure support from individuals outside the company, individuals like me.

While celebrated in movies and televisions ads, the lone cowboy is a desolate figure when trouble strikes. Bereft, too, is the solo colleague separated from the workforce. Listen to Catherine Bergart, who lost her advertising job during the downturn. "I not only lost my income but I also lost a day-to-day camaraderie of a particularly close group of colleagues," she told *The New York Times*. Now isolated at home as a freelance writer, she finds herself depressed. She struggles to keep a sense of perspective and humor about her life.[2]

Psychologists confirm that being alone during a crisis carries inherent risks. After the US Airways flight crashed in the Hudson River, for example, Kenneth Manges, a clinical psychologist in Cincinnati who has treated survivors of floods, fires, and armed robberies, said, "People who are isolated are at risk for post-traumatic stress."[3] Steven Daviss, chair of the psychology department at Baltimore Washington Medical Center, advises those struggling with the economic downturn "not to go it alone. . . . There are lots of other people in the same boat, getting together to talk things out, not just to commiserate but to help problem-solve."[4]

We see crisis support systems at work all around us. When police get in trouble trying to apprehend criminals, they call for backup. NFL head football coaches depend on other coaches who are seated high above the field to pass down plays and formations during the game through the head coach's headset. EMTs rarely make a solo rescue; instead, they routinely work with a partner. Even on television, the buddy system rules. In *Who Wants to Be a Millionaire?*, a contestant can employ a "lifeline" by calling a trusted friend when stumped by a question. In fact, he or she has the option to poll the whole studio audience for answers. Securing support is a smart response to life's challenges.

Propping Up One Another

Max Cleland was a shining example of the self-reliant man. He served in the U.S. Army during the Vietnam War, rising to the rank of captain.

He was awarded the Bronze Star for meritorious service and the Silver Star for gallantry in combat. With just a month left in his tour, Cleland jumped out of a helicopter near Khe Sanh on April 8, 1968, and spotted a grenade he believed he had dropped. He attempted to retrieve it. The grenade exploded.

In his book *Heart of a Patriot*, Cleland describes the frequent conversation he had with himself after the grenade blast left him with two leg stumps and an arm stump: "Cleland, you are dumb. You've screwed everything up. You blew yourself up. You've ruined your life and your body. You're just a dumbass."[5] Cleland faced a mammoth task: learning to forgive himself. When I met Max in 2010, he told me he grew up with a very "egocentric personality": if anything went wrong he blamed himself, while he took credit for whatever went right.

The Snake Pit

The army sent the injured Cleland to the Walter Reed Medical Center outside Washington, DC, for rehabilitation. He joined a group of officers who'd also lost limbs in Vietnam. "We were all young. Young eagles, young strapping tigers, and we all had lost something . . . we had lost time, we had lost energy. We had lost, in many ways, faith, and we had lost parts of our physical bodies which was the focus at that moment." Max told me that he and his fellow officers were huddled together in beds at the end of a cul-de-sac of an old corridor. A snake motif slithered along the mosaic on the ceramic floor of their ward. Hence, they dubbed their home away from home the "Snake Pit."

Max said the wounded officers identified with each other not just as individuals but also as a group. "We were all in this boat together. We were all struggling with physical therapy. We were all struggling with Walter Reed and getting to the chow hall and . . . fascinated by the young physical therapists, nurses, and ladies."

Max said he survived his injuries because of this small "band of brothers. If you started crying at night and sobbing, you knew that those guys were there and that they were hearing you. They didn't say anything . . . and then when others sobbed, you were with them . . . so one day you're the helped and the next day you're the helper." Max also said that they teased and challenged each other and misbehaved like college students. One of the injured officers arranged for a stripper to come to the Snake Pit. She snuck past the night desk wearing a raincoat and then disrobed, revealing a scanty outfit, before she launched into singing "The Star Spangled Banner."[6] Cleland's role as a ringleader of fellow amputees at Walter Reed hospital helped him fend off depression.

After eight months in the Snake Pit, Max "graduated" to a nearby VA hospital and then, once he demonstrated he could take care of himself, to a tiny studio apartment near Walter Reed. While he enjoyed being back in charge of his life, he was now alone. Instead of twenty-four-hour companionship with other veterans, his companions became Beatles music and alcohol. "The only thing I had in my icebox was Wild Turkey. And then I had daiquiri mix on the counter. That was it . . . booze was certainly an attractive outlet and escape. . . . The instinct is to drink your way out of it."

Years later, Max's over-enjoyment of alcohol had not ended. He joined a female friend who was going to Alcoholics Anonymous. He didn't think he had a drinking problem, but he was struck by the powerful stories of personal loss he heard from AA members. "Loss of integrity, loss of sanity, loss of status, loss of, I mean you just name it. Hurting others, being impacted by that. All of that hell that you are not supposed to do but end up doing anyway is revealed in the alcoholic's story."

Max said he had never been in such an honest environment, and it was the only form of "counseling" he had received since the grenade blast. He spent two and a half years at Al-Anon talking about his own pain and moving through the 12-step program. He said he realized that he had begun to like alcohol too much and that he didn't want to drink anymore or be around those who did. The Al-Anon group provided his first real postwar "counseling." He successfully quit drinking.

Trained Not to Share

Just as important, Max worked on the guilt, pain, and blame that he carried with him, beginning the process of moving beyond his injury. "Military people are trained not to share. I mean, it's a sign of weakness. They're trained not to break down. They are trained not to accept the fact that they might have screwed up, and somewhere along the line, they're in a bind. They are not trained to go to a group setting." By sharing his tale of loss, Max realized "the world is not going to come to an end." Once you understand this, Max explains, "then you try to move on."

Max was appointed head of the U.S. Veterans Administration and elected Secretary of State of Georgia before being elected to the U.S. Senate in 1996. His love for the Senate was short-lived, like his former "young strapping tiger's" body. When Max ran for reelection in 2002, his opponent's campaign ads questioned his patriotism and linked him to Osama Bin Laden. Max lost his reelection bid.

Max told me he started crying after the election and kept crying on and off for the next two and a half years as depression set in. Max felt he had lost everything because of his defeat: his identity, his job, his staff, and his income. Fortunately, a U.S. Navy psychiatrist introduced him to another 12-step program, this one for high-profile Washingtonians whose lives had flamed out. Nicknamed "the last house on the block," the group of disaffected "big shots"—congresspeople and ex-congresspeople, admirals and ex-admirals, senators and ex-senators—met weekly. "All of us have crashed and burned for whatever reason—drugs, alcohol, sex, power, depression, whatever—but we've all crashed and burned . . . we've all come as close as you can come to not being there. Some in the room had come close in putting a gun to their head, but didn't pull the trigger. This isn't just group therapy, this is fighting for your life, and everybody there understands that."

When he joined the group, Max said that he had never felt worse in his entire life, including getting blown up. So he spilled his guts to the group for several years. "I don't care what kind of a group it is, if you're in a group that knows you and loves you and accepts you, and you're able to be honest with them, that is very empowering." Yet the group alone wasn't enough to end Max's severe depression.

Take Control of Your Past

Max found a trauma counselor at Walter Reed. Together they focused on his need to take control of his past rather than letting it dictate his future. His counselor calls it "the trail of trauma." Now Max sees himself in the process of recovery for the rest of his life, not only from alcohol but also from a series of life crises. He has already made major progress in coming to terms with his life. Perhaps a catalyst in this process was the 1998 admission of a former U.S. Vietnam soldier who stepped forward to confess that he had dropped the hand grenade that blew up Max Cleland.

•   •   •

When we suffer a personal crisis, we may rely on high-profile groups outside our own circle that can help us become Instant Survivors: Alcoholics Anonymous, Al-Anon, American Cancer Society, Susan G. Komen for the Cure, American Red Cross. Legions of people have benefited by creating or joining groups of people who suffer the same affliction they do.

A recent example of a support group for the financially traumatized is the Madoff Survivor's Group. After the Bernie Madoff Ponzi scheme scandal, some of his victims created this web forum, which allows them to trade hardship stories, compare notes about claims and tax issues, and support and encourage one another.[7]

In Palo Alto, California, teens bonded to ease each other's pain in the wake of suicides at The Henry M. Gunn High School. A group of students created T-shirts carrying the message "Talk to Me" and formed pacts not to harm themselves. Another group posted inspirational notes of optimism throughout the campus.[8]

Jonny Imerman is a survivor of testicular cancer. His nonprofit, Imerman Angels, has recruited more than two thousand cancer survivors as volunteer mentors for new cancer patients. His goal is to create a wide network of testicular cancer survivors so that within twenty-four hours of diagnosis a new patient can be in touch with a survivor. "It's very different than another friend, who might be sympathetic but just can't understand from personal experience," Matt Ferstler, an Austin, Texas, cancer survivor told the *Wall Street Journal.* Ferstler said that he could talk with the mentor about his true concerns. "Am I going to be able to have a normal sex life? Will someone accept me if I'm different?"[9]

Social networking groups have formed to address parenthood challenges. Last year there were nearly eighty thousand different "parents groups" on Yahoo alone. Groups exist for pregnant women, parents of autistic children, and single parents.[10]

Finally, imagine the struggle of Taryn Davis, who married at age nineteen. Eighteen months later her soldier husband, Michael, was killed in Iraq by a roadside bomb. She tried attending a local grief group for those who'd lost spouses to disease, but they were much older than she was. She told *People* magazine: "I wanted to meet widows who would share with me how they met their husbands, how they fell in love, how they dealt with his deployment—and most importantly, what makes them get up every day and find a reason to live." She traveled around the country meeting other young military widows and posted videos on her website, www.americanwidowproject.org. She and other military widows now attend six getaways a year, full of celebration and heart-to-heart talks.[11]

We've all heard about the "fight-or-flight" battle we face when threatened. Our brain stems may direct us to retreat, go into a shell, and face a disaster alone. We also are excellent at manufacturing reasons why we shouldn't ask others for help: "I don't want to bother them"; "I don't want their pity"; or "They can't or don't want to help me."

Your Greatest Anchor in a Crisis

How can we combat our reluctance to ask others for help? Recognize their value. Dr. Phil McGraw told *Parade* magazine, "Your loved ones can be your greatest anchor in a crisis—if you let them."[12] Another important step is to ask for help before we really need it. You already have a crisis management plan. Now you need a crisis management team that will be ready to help you put your plan into action.

Creating a team that includes your friends and relatives will also make crises easier on them. Oftentimes, these support people struggle to help another family member or friend in crisis because they themselves find it so hard to cope. "Most people cannot tolerate the feeling of helplessness," Jackson Rainer, a professor of psychology at Georgia Southern University who has studied grief and relationships, told *The New York Times*. "And in the presence of another's crisis, there's always the sense of helplessness."[13] Making the people close to you part of a team committed to working from a crisis management plan will make it easier for them to help you. Remind them, too, that you are part of their go-to team should they need support, advice, or counsel one day.

Instant Survivor™ Alert

Let's assemble your own crisis management team right now. Secure for yourself the support you either need at this moment or will need in order to face a future disaster.

Focus first on who should be the "insiders" and "outsiders" on your crisis management team. Insiders are family members and close friends who care about you and will be useful in a pinch. Outsiders will be specialists you can call on, such as a lawyer or an accountant, depending on the type of crisis.

MANAGER TIP #4—ONE IS THE LONELIEST NUMBER

If you have a colleague who is suffering a personal or professional crisis, ask him or her this question:

What friends or group can help you get through what you're going through?

Think hard as you make the list, which should total no more than five or six people. Have you been to these people for advice before? Do they listen well? Have they been helpful to you in the past? Are they thoughtful, generous, and calm under pressure? Do they truly care about you? Will they tell you things for your own good that you may not want to hear? If so, ask them to join your team. Sure, it'll sound a little weird to them, but blame it on the advice I've given you. Flatter them that you want them because you know they can and will help. And so they don't think it'll be an extra full-time job, explain that you'll call on them only if real trouble strikes. If you feel shy about asking for their support, start by pledging to be there for them if they find themselves in their darkest hour. Tell them you want them to be part of your "medical" team—to diagnose whatever problem comes up, to treat the symptoms, to find the root causes, and to help find a cure.

Now add the outsiders. They can't be strangers; preferably, they should

ONE IS THE LONELIEST NUMBER

- Create a crisis management team before you need it.
- Rely on various groups for support.
- Select a variety of individuals, professionals, friends, and business associates to be part of your team.
- Your loved ones are your greatest anchor in a crisis.

be professionals you've employed previously (such as your accountant or tax return preparer, or maybe a lawyer who's a good generalist—not a wonk in an obscure legal niche). Explain to them you want them on the team because they're sharp, not for specific professional advice. The idea is to balance the team with people who have a blood or pure friendship connection to you and professionals who will lend a more unbiased perspective to handling tricky situations.

Put the complete contact information of all team members on a single page and distribute it to the team. Tell them you'll give them a copy of the plan when you have it ready. This will reassure them that you're taking this project seriously and help guide them to be helpful to you. (I kind of tricked you. Once you promise them a plan, at least one of the team members will pester you until you cough it up.) *The Instant Survivor™* Handbook, which you can download for free at www.instantsurvivor. com, contains a crisis management team template for you.

•   •   •

My career is actually based on being part of a crisis management team. Clients hire me to work with others from both inside and outside the company to deal with a crisis. When I faced my own personal crisis, I drew on that firsthand experience to build my own crisis management team. Once my team was in place, I did not stand still; I took decisive action to confront the trouble facing me.

5

NO STANDING STILL

How often have you quoted or heard quoted the law of a man named Murphy whom you've never met? We've all heard it: "Anything that can go wrong will go wrong." But you may not have heard one of the corollaries of Murphy's Law: "Left to themselves, things tend to go from bad to worse."

Remember Lehman Brothers, the investment bank that collapsed in 2008? For several years, it had been the smallest of the major independent investment banks, a precarious position for a global financial services operation requiring vast capital and competing against behemoths. For CEO Dick Fuld, however, staying independent—not being swallowed by a large insurance company or bank or other financial services conglomerate—was the Holy Grail.

So with Fuld at the helm, Lehman Brothers navigated several other earlier stock market disasters that might have brought it down. In the two years before its demise, perhaps feeling invincible, Fuld led Lehman to borrow heavily to invest in commercial real estate (despite red flag warnings about the faltering market).

Fuld finally woke up after another independent investment bank, Bear Stearns, cratered in early 2008. Fuld began shopping for companies to buy all or parts of Lehman. It was too late and he asked for too much money. Regulators refused to rescue the bank. Lehman died in September 2008, having neither reached his Holy Grail nor saved his followers along the way.[1]

Fuld overplayed a weak hand. Job one for a CEO—and for us—is survival. Fuld could have saved Lehman and its employees with an earlier sale to a larger financial services firm. He treated his goal of continued independence for Lehman as a *sound strategy* when it was really an *unrealistic aspiration*. Delay in finding a home left Lehman homeless—and bankrupt.

How often have we learned the harsh lesson that, like unharvested fruit, untended problems turn rotten? When our relationships sour, they get worse unless we actively work to improve them. Our health problems, such as illnesses, rashes, or sprains, routinely turn menacing when we ignore them. Likewise, our financial problems, such as missed mortgage payments, unpaid credit cards, or calls from creditors, are dismissed at our peril.

Do we continue to gain weight when we fail to exercise and eat sensibly? Do our debts grow if left unmanaged? Does an addiction—to alcohol, drugs, gambling—worsen without intervention? The answer to all three questions is, of course, yes. In so many life situations, *inaction creates devastation*. What keeps us from responding to trouble? We deny its existence, we worry instead of acting, and we allow fear to keep us immobile.

Denial

If this is so, why do we delay action? The first reason is denial. We are surrounded by crisis every day. When we listen to the radio, open the newspaper, or overhear a conversation at a restaurant, we hear about the economic crisis, energy crisis, climate crisis, health crisis, banking crisis, drug crisis, obesity crisis, and confidence crisis. We turn on the TV to find armchair experts hotly debating the origins of and solutions to these crises. We live in a world of crisis overdose.

We get to a point where we hear about so many crises that we ignore them. We go into a state of denial. What can we do about the financial crisis anyway? We respond to hearing about the latest crisis with a shrug. We donate a few dollars to the victims of the latest natural disaster, and we go back to a state of inaction.

You can survive and even thrive by denying national and worldwide crises. Yet there is one crisis, whether current or incoming, that you cannot deny. *Your* crisis. You cannot deny it, and you must take immediate action to deal with it. Because if you don't, no one will.

It is our human nature to assume that bad things will happen to others, not to us. We can't help being human.

Take divorce, job loss, scandal, disabling injury, early death of a child, AIDS. These calamities will hit neighbors, coworkers, politicians. Celebrities' lives, too, seem rife with downfalls, but us? Recent surveys show that people think they are 49 percent less likely than others to get divorced, are 32 percent less likely to be fired, and are even 12 percent less likely to get gum disease.[2]

For thirty years, family, friends, neighbors, coworkers, executives, and politicians have shared with me what they think in general about their troubles, whether a crisis is looming in the distance or right on their doorstep. Most of them, like the rest of us, deny that they will face a crisis in the future. If life is going well, people prefer to assume that it will always go well.

Isn't that how you think? We all do. In fact, psychiatrists have a term for it: "discounting."

Even when a crisis first hits, we keep the denial button pressed down. We reckon it will quickly pass by and that trying to solve it will make it worse. We assert that it's not really happening. To be an *Instant Survivor*™, though, we have to learn to work through this denial, accept the reality of the situation, and take immediate, positive action.

Worry

When we face a crisis, we feel lost, without a playbook, beset by fear, doubt, worry, and dread. Alone in the car at a stoplight, in the shower, as we walk the dog, as we stare at the ceiling after turning the lights out, we obsess about it.

Maybe we talk about it with a best friend, spouse, or sibling on the phone or at the kitchen table. Too often, however, we're afraid to talk to anyone, so we persist in scary, solo struggles. While we're paralyzed by panic, the passage of time doesn't improve our situations. A new job doesn't materialize out of nowhere. A recurring pain in the lower abdomen doesn't suddenly disappear. A torn-up marriage doesn't magically mend.

Life is terrifying when it ambushes us. Dozens of desperate faces stared back at me when I told a company's employees they were being laid off. They were frantic because they had no plan in place to confront their crisis. A year later, fear gripped me, too, when I found myself in similar straits.

Like denial, worry causes us to avoid action. Worry actually serves as a substitute for action. When we worry about a crisis, we feel like we are doing something about it when actually we are not. Excess worry inhibits our ability to take action. As we face a crisis en route to being an *Instant Survivor*™, we must learn to overcome worry, just as we overcome denial, by securing support.

"Everybody lies."

When we succumb to denial and excess worry, we begin to lie to ourselves. As TV's Dr. House says in the series *House*, "Everybody lies." Let's be more generous and just say we tend to delay dealing with our problems with a series of excuses: "It will get better." "It's not that bad."

"It will blow over." "I'll ride it out." "I'll only make it worse if I try to fix it." "I'll decide what to do when I know more." Psychologists categorize some of us as "ambivalent" (as opposed to being decisive), which means we are more prone to avoid making decisions and to stay longer in unhappy relationships.[3] Of course, there are situations when doing nothing makes sense, such as when an injury will heal itself without the risk of surgery. But doing nothing is rarely the right way to respond when problems are serious.

You don't have to be an engineer to know that a plane's forward momentum during flight is crucial, that a stall in midair, when engine power is cut, can mean a nose-diving plane and death. Beware going into "stall" mode during a crisis. Winston Churchill summed up the situation nicely: "When you are going through hell, by all means keep going."

Would Isabel Gillies have rebuilt a new life for herself and her children if she had stayed put? Would Diane Rehm's voice have improved if she hadn't persisted in her search for an accurate diagnosis?

In 2001, *American Idol* judge Randy Jackson was forty-five years old, weighed 360 pounds, and was in the worst shape of his life. His father was a diabetic who took insulin shots. Jackson wrote in his book, *Body with Soul*, "For five long days I had been feeling sick in the craziest kind of way—extremely tired, extremely thirsty, all sweaty and dizzy."

Jackson's doctor told him to meet him in the emergency room. Nurses checked Jackson's blood pressure and tested the level of sugar in his blood. The doctor told his patient, "You have Type 2 diabetes. Your blood sugar is over five hundred."[4] Blood sugar readings should be in the low hundreds.

Delay Is Typical

Even though he had a diabetic father, Jackson had put off a trip to the doctor before being properly diagnosed and treated for a disease that affects an estimated twenty-one million Americans.

Jackson's slow response to his health issue was typical and occurs in response to small and huge problems alike. We become comfortable in our lives, even when we're unhappy or unhealthy, and we often delay taking action and securing support until looming disaster prompts us to change.

The TV show *The Biggest Loser* highlights the downside of delay. In case you haven't seen it, the program is a weight-loss competition, combined with the vote-off-the-island feature of the equally popular reality show *Survivor*. The contestants, selected from around the country, face weight crises: they are obese and have been unable to lose weight on their own. They move away from home for several months while trainers control their diets and enforce a rugged exercise regimen.

Feel Alive Again

The physical transformations of the participants during the course of the show are stunning; they are often unrecognizable in their "after" pictures. One winner lost 58 percent of her body weight, with several others close behind. Even more amazing is the mental transformations the contestants achieve. Ali Vincent, who lost 112 pounds and was the first female winner, told *The National Ledger*, "I don't know when I forgot I was a strong, capable woman. I awoke the athlete in me. I feel alive again."[5]

A recent *People* magazine article chronicled the weight-loss saga of a British teenager. Georgia Davis, five feet seven inches, from Aberdare, Wales, said in a typical day she would eat a loaf of bread and could wolf down half a pie in one sitting. She weighed 464 pounds and said she "saw my life going nowhere." Doctors told her that if she didn't lose weight, she'd die, and in 2007, she was diagnosed with diabetes. The UK press called her "Britain's fattest teen."

Only then did she "decide to take control of my life instead of ruining it." She left her home and for nine months joined a North Carolina weight-loss boarding school. Imagine the courage it took for a fifteen-year-old to leave her family and friends, travel across the ocean to a foreign country, and live there among strangers for close to a year. She lost 202 pounds and no longer has diabetes. She told the interviewer, "Now I see my life going somewhere . . . I can go to college; I can have someone special; I can have kids. . . . Being here has given me my life back."[6]

Yes, Georgia ultimately triumphed. However, she might have had a happier childhood, focused on other life ambitions, and avoided the pain and agony of her weight-cycle trauma if she had faced up to addressing her weight gain much earlier. Securing support became essential when her obesity threatened her life.

Georgia's story illuminates how delay traps so many of us in poor health and pain before seven alarm bells of danger spark us into action and into transforming ourselves, physically and mentally. While *The Biggest Loser* creates many winners, who shed enormous weight and capture new hope through the help of others, potential "winners" among us remain weighed down by health, financial, relationship, and job troubles we have let fester.

Listen to General Douglas MacArthur about the fatal consequences of delay: "The history of the failure of war can almost be summed up in two words: too late.

- Too late in comprehending the deadly purpose of a potential enemy.

- Too late in realizing the mortal danger.

- Too late in preparedness.

- Too late in uniting all possible forces for resistance.

- Too late in standing with one's friends."[7]

Let's look at more examples of delay—often triggered by arrogance and pride—that were lethal for reputations, and lives.

Too Little, Too Late

In August 2000, the Russian submarine *Kursk* exploded and sank during a military exercise with 118 sailors on board. The Russians made three rescue attempts. All failed. Meanwhile, Russian President Vladimir Putin refused offers of assistance from other countries. Four days after the sub sank, Putin finally accepted help from the Royal Navy. When the submarine hatch was opened, the rescuers discovered that all the sailors had perished. How many lives might have been saved had Putin immediately accepted outside offers to help with the search and rescue?

At 7:15 a.m. on a spring day in 2007, Virginia Tech police reported to the university's president and other senior administrators the shooting of two students on campus. The response: lock down the dormitory where the shooting occurred. But those administrators relied on a mistaken report that the shooter had left the campus and that police were questioning a "person of interest." Neither students nor faculty were notified about the early-morning shootings until an e-mail was sent out over two hours later—far too late to stop thirty additional murders in a science building just minutes after that notice was sent. A delayed response based on bad assumptions and wrong facts proved deadly.

It seems obvious: delay is destructive, but immediate action can short-circuit trouble. The Chinese philosopher Lao-Tzu said, simply, "The biggest problem in the world could have been solved when it was small." Let's move past our pride and arrogance, which keep us in stall mode and prevent us from securing support. Let's remind ourselves of the dangers that lie on the other side of delay—hard lessons learned by Lehman Brothers CEO Dick Fuld, the "Biggest Losers," Russian President Vladimir Putin, Virginia Tech officials, and many others. Let's ditch our excuses to delay taking action *right now* to resolve our problems. Heed the advice of President Teddy Roosevelt: "In the moment of decision the best thing to do is the right thing; the worst thing to do is nothing."

Instant Survivor™ Alert

Think of something you are delaying right now. It doesn't matter whether it has to do with your personal or your professional life. Are you putting off making that awkward phone call to a client? The call to your doctor for an overdue physical? The e-mail to your friend explaining that you have to drop out of your neighborhood association? The conversation with your boss about the new competition?

MANAGER TIP #5—NO STANDING STILL

If you have a colleague who is suffering a personal or professional crisis, ask him or her this question:

What do you think happens if you delay taking action to address it?

Now take action. Pick up the phone. Write that e-mail. Walk over to your boss's office. After you have done that, sit down and write out a list of what might have happened if you had not taken action. Then follow that list with a list of what happened because you took action.

Study the difference. Are you convinced that you are risking a lot by not taking action?

Can you recall suffering a professional or personal crisis in which you did not take action?

And remind yourself, as the folks we learned about in this chapter did, to rely on your support network and accept their offers to help you take action.

NO STANDING STILL

Standing still in response to a crisis can be dangerous to your health. Instead, follow some key steps of *The Instant Survivor™* System:

- Move beyond a state of denial.

- Stop substituting worry for action.

- Stop telling lies about your situation.

- Accept help from others to tackle your problems.

• • •

Once you learn to take immediate action and accept help from others, you will avoid the "too late" syndrome that explains most military, professional, and personal defeats. Taking immediate action demands that you maintain visibility during your crisis. As we will discuss in the next chapter, going underground is not an option. Well, at least not a good option.

DON'T HIDE

Michael Dell revolutionized the sale of personal computers. Until the early 1980s, only retail stores sold personal computers. Operating out of a condominium, Dell started selling PCs directly to consumers. In 1992, at the age of twenty-seven, he was the youngest CEO to have his company ranked in *Fortune* magazine's "Best of the Top 500" corporations.

Around that time, a technology conference scheduled him as a speaker. The day before the conference, Dell's computer company announced surprisingly poor results. The stock plunged. The moderator of the conference assumed Michael Dell wouldn't show up, but he not only appeared but also acted unconcerned, and he reassured investors by calmly explaining his business plan.[1]

Dell followed a key crisis management principle: *stay visible when there's trouble.*

While you may accept the wisdom of that principle for companies, you may wonder how and why it applies to you. You may be thinking, "Well, Michael Dell had to show up. He's the CEO of the company." Since you may not be an elected politician, appointed big shot, or a high-ranking company or organizational officer, you may feel you don't need to stay visible during your crisis.

In fact, you may feel that when you face a disaster it's okay to drop out of sight. To hide. To lie low. To fade to black. To be missing in action. You may think that Woody Allen's approach to death makes sense for you during your professional or personal trauma: "I'm not afraid of it. I just don't want to be around when it happens."

We Are Leaders

But we are leaders. We need to "lead" ourselves out of our own hardships. Plus, family members, friends, coworkers, and other acquaintances rely on us. Even if our job titles may not bill us as leaders and our community of contacts may be small, we own the title of leader because people depend on us.

Think what happens when you fade from view during times of trouble. Your friends know that something is wrong in your life. If you suddenly become invisible, they will assume the worst: you must be in really bad shape to disappear on them. Absence doesn't make the heart grow fonder; it makes the rumors grow stronger. Your allies may conclude that you are a wimp. The people they admire in life run to trouble, not away from it. Leaders maintain their poise despite defeat, disappointment, and despair.

Think about why it's so reassuring when a leader stays visible during a calamity. A leader demonstrates psychological strength, control over events, and focus on a solution. A leader secures support through the courage he or she demonstrates.

I recently helped a friend of mine who had lost his job. He told me he was spending about 75 percent of his time pursuing jobs online and only 25 percent of his time networking.

I advised him to reverse those percentages. One of the keys to success in life is sharing your efforts and success with others. If you are cooped up at home tied to your computer, sending out résumés that aren't read, your job search will founder. Plus, your allies won't feel invested in your job search, and if they don't hear from you they'll assume that you're just sitting at home, depressed, watching TV. By calling his friends and by using social networks to energize his relationships, my friend found a job he's excited about within a month of our conversation.

As we secure support, we must become leaders, even if we are homeless and living in a parking lot.

"My home is a Walmart parking lot."

Brianna Karp lost her job as an executive assistant in July 2008. She lasted for a while on temp jobs and unemployment benefits but couldn't continue to pay her rent. So, she moved into a truck and camper she had inherited from her father, who had committed suicide. Karp pulled the camper into a Walmart parking lot and lived there for months.

If anyone had an excuse to lie low as her life nose-dived, it was Karp. But instead, she started blogging from a nearby coffee shop on a blogspot she titled *The Girl's Guide to Homelessness*. Her posts were an upbeat and engaging chronicle of her life. "I was trying to stay positive and cheerful," Karp told CNN. "I started writing a blog in a tongue-in-cheek way to kind of laugh about my circumstances . . . I didn't think anyone would actually read it."

Karp also applied for a job with *Elle* magazine advice columnist E. Jean Carroll and won an internship. Carroll told CNN she was intrigued by Karp's e-mail to her, which began, "Dear E. Jean: I'm currently homeless and living in a Walmart parking lot. I'm educated, I've never done drugs, and I'm not mentally ill. I have a strong employment history and I'm a career executive assistant. The instability sucks, but I'm rocking it as best I can."[2] Karp's blog kept her visible, attracted attention, secured support, and helped rejuvenate her life.

Work Hard to Be Seen

Let's take a page from this nation's history. One of the bleakest periods during the American Revolutionary War was the winter our soldiers spent in Valley Forge, Pennsylvania. They had little to eat, little to wear, and lived in crowded, freezing, damp huts. Washington wrote that without money his army faced three choices: "starve, dissolve, or disperse."[3]

Where was General George Washington at the time? Right there with his troops at Valley Forge.

In December 1776, the American Continental Army suffered a series of defeats and retreated south from New York to Baltimore in the face of advancing British troops. General Washington's remaining troops were cold, exhausted, and short on supplies. Washington wrote, "I'm wearied almost to death with the retrograde motion of things."[4] Washington engineered a surprise attack on the British troops at Trenton, New Jersey, inspiring the famous painting of him standing in a boat crossing the Delaware River to lead the attack. Washington's bold pose embodies the value of visibility in the midst of a crisis.

Instant Survivor™ Alert

How can you be a leader during a disaster? How can you reassure those who love, like, and know you that you are in control, taking your problem in stride, and moving ahead with your life? Multiply your regular routine. Work hard to be seen even more where you shop, where your kids go to school, and where you stop for coffee. Lend a bigger hand to your favorite charity. Join an exercise group or a book club. Give people a chance to see you in action, acting normally. Being visible helps cement your support.

MANAGER TIP #6—DON'T HIDE

If you have a colleague who is suffering a personal or professional crisis, ask him or her this question:

How can you stay visible to reassure your friends and allies that you will survive this challenge?

Do it whether you're getting divorced, looking for a new job, confronting a disease, or hurting financially. Of course, I know all this is more easily said than done. When we get clocked by a problem, we feel depressed, tired, and beaten. Pulling the covers over our head is what we want to do when a bad blow shakes our self-confidence. So why is it so important to force ourselves to stay visible?

YOU WILL WIN NEW RESPECT. Your courage will gain you new respect and new friends. Everybody admires someone who stands up to trouble.

YOU WILL GET MORE HELP. You make it easier for others to help you move past your own problem when they see you staying on track with your life. The more pain and strain you show, the harder you make it for those around you to help, because they feel helpless in the face of your plight. Think about your own experience. Don't you find it easier to assist someone who is taking charge and pushing past problems rather than acting like a sniveling basket case?

YOU WILL SET A GREAT EXAMPLE. Define yourself in a crisis, don't let a crisis define you. When you take a hit, everyone watches to see your reaction. Will you stay down or get back up? When you're brave, you encourage others to emulate the behavior you've modeled when they take a knock. Albert Einstein said, "Setting an example is not the main means of influencing another, it is the only means."[5] Fighting through what ails you is a great lesson for your colleagues, family members, and your friends.

DON'T HIDE

Step forward, not back, in a crisis. In essence you're saying, "Hey, everybody, look at me!"

- Win new respect.
- Get more help from allies.
- Set a great example.
- Feel better about how you're handling trouble.

YOU WILL FEEL BETTER. Getting out and about will help give you perspective on your problem and will keep you in social contact, which is critical when you're down. Slouching around solo can trigger a downward spiral of self-pity, sadness, and submission.

If you're in the midst of a disaster, avoid being alone in dark places. Find the light outside. Feel the warmth of friends. Enjoy the spotlight of being courageous in a crisis. You will tighten your circle of support.

•   •   •

Stepping forward to secure support requires that you take responsibility for your actions. This sometimes entails facing up to the tough task of making an apology when necessary.

APOLOGIZE

When Dick Fuld, the Lehman Brothers CEO I discussed in chapter five, appeared in front of a congressional committee, he suggested the blame for Lehman's downfall rested with everyone but himself. Fuld blamed rumors, misguided regulators, accounting rules, and a "storm of fear" on Wall Street.[1] Although Fuld was constrained in what he could say because of lawsuits filed against Lehman and him, it would have been possible for him to express regret without increasing his litigation exposure. His unrepentant tone and attitude further undermined his reputation.

Unlike Dick Fuld, John J. Mack, CEO of investment bank Morgan Stanley, didn't duck when he testified in front of Congress in early 2009 about his bank's role in the financial crisis. "We are sorry for it," he said simply.[2]

The Time Warner–AOL merger was another disastrous failure. Jerry Levin, Time Warner's former chief executive, penitently told CNBC, "I'm really very sorry about the pain and suffering and loss caused. . . . I presided over the worst deal of the century. . . . It is time for those involved in companies to stand up and say, 'You know what, I am solely responsible for it, I was the CEO, I was in charge.'"[3] While late in coming, at least Mr. Levin's apology was full-throated, complete, and apparently genuine.

As the above examples show, making an immediate apology is a key component of corporate crisis management. Making an apology solidifies support and puts the corporation on a path to positive action.

Apology Report Card

It's just as important for you to make any necessary apologies as you deal with your personal and professional crises. Let's take a look at some recent apologies made by individuals and grade them as a way to understand more completely when apologies work and when they don't. What is a good apology versus a bad one? When is one mangled and why?

Grade: F

Jean Washington is a cleaning worker in a Maryland courthouse south of Washington, DC. She arrives for her shift in the middle of the afternoon and likes to park her car close to the courthouse because her shift typically ends at 8:30 p.m., and she doesn't want to walk far to her car in the dark. One of the courthouse judges is Robert C. Nalley, who was upset that courthouse workers like Ms. Washington were parking in a restricted area.

One afternoon Ms. Washington took a call from a sheriff's deputy who warned her that some man was letting air out of her tire.[4] She rushed to the parking lot, but it was too late; her tire was flat. She burst into tears. The man who had flattened her tire? Judge Nalley.[5]

"No Big Deal"

After an article about the incident appeared in the local newspaper a couple of days later, Judge Nalley admitted to a supervising judge that he had deflated the tire, but told the supervisor that he didn't think it was a "big deal." Nalley apologized to his supervisor, not for flattening the tire but for not notifying him about the matter earlier.[6] Several days later Judge Nalley's supervisor reported that Nalley was "very chagrined. He feels embarrassed because he did it and now he's placed the court in a bad light."[7]

Nalley was suspended from sitting on criminal cases until after the incident was resolved. At a hearing several months later, he pleaded guilty to tampering with a motor vehicle. The sentencing judge gave Nalley probation before judgment, so that he would avoid a conviction on his record if he successfully completed the terms of probation. He was also fined $500 and ordered to write a "heartfelt" letter of apology to Ms. Washington.[8] Waiting until you are ordered by a court of law to make an apology wins you only one prize—for being far too late.

Grade: D+ (for Delay)

Sometimes we are called on to apologize for things that occurred long ago but still rankle those who were wronged. Malaga Island, near Sebasco, Maine, was a year-round fishing community of forty black, white, and mixed-raced residents whose composition had a history of upsetting other Maine locals.

In 1911, the State of Maine bought the island and started a relocation process that moved eight of its residents to the Maine School for the Feeble-Minded in New Gloucester and forcibly evicted every other resident of the island, by orders of the governor. State officials took down and relocated the island schoolhouse, then dug up the seventeen bodies in the island cemetery and reburied them in five graves at the mental institution. Several of the islanders spent the rest of their lives at that state-run facility.

Waiting for a Century

Not until a century later did the State of Maine issue a public apology. Maine lawmakers passed a unanimous joint resolution to apologize as the 2010 legislative session was coming to a close. The weird part: the legislators didn't tell anybody that the apology was coming, nor did they announce they had made it. No press release. No website announcement. Nothing. Message sent, but not delivered.

"All I can say is that I am glad, glad, glad it was done, but it was really a disservice to the descendants," said Marilyn Darling Voter, whose great-great-grandfather's sisters, nieces, and nephews were evicted from Malaga Island. As she told the *Down East* magazine reporter, "It's one thing to write all that out and acknowledge it—we did this and that—but it's like reading it with your back turned. There should have been somebody there to say 'you are forgiven' or 'we accept' or 'about time.'"[9] You can't make an effective apology and keep it a secret.

Why did the State of Maine have to wait one hundred years to apologize to the descendants of the former residents of Malaga Island? Perhaps its legislators did not realize that even a short delay on the path to apology can undercut its value to nearly nil.

Grade: D

When Mel Gibson was arrested in the summer of 2006 for drunk driving, he made vicious anti-Semitic statements to the Los Angeles County sheriff's deputies who arrested him. Gibson's relations with the Jewish community had been clouded since his 2004 film, *The Passion of the Christ*, which many Jews felt unfairly portrayed the role of Jews in the crucifixion of Jesus. As a result, Gibson's rant to the deputies reignited a storm of criticism from Jewish groups.

Gibson's statement the day after his arrest noted that he had "said things that I did not believe to be true and which are despicable."[10]

His statement failed to address his anti-Semitic remarks, though, and only several days later did Gibson issue a second statement in which he clearly stated, "I want to apologize to everyone in the Jewish community for the vitriolic and harmful words that I said to a law enforcement officer the night I was arrested on a DUI charge."[11] Gibson's slow response solidified the presumption of many that he holds anti-Semitic views.

Grade: C-

Remember how tennis star Serena Williams berated a linesperson at the U.S. Open in 2009? In a semifinal match, Serena was serving at 5–6, 15–30 in the second set when a linesperson called a foot fault on her second serve (which meant Serena lost the point). Serena twice approached the linesperson, cursing and shaking her racket at her, including a threat to shove "the f***ing ball down [the linesperson's] f***ing throat." The umpire then docked Serena for unsportsmanlike conduct and issued a penalty point against her (Serena had been forewarned after an earlier display of temper), ending the match in favor of Serena's opponent.[12]

In a press conference after the Saturday match, Serena was unrepentant and unyielding when asked about the incident.

Q. Do you think the lineswoman deserves an apology?
A. An apology for?
Q. From you.
A. From me? Well, how many people yell at linespeople?[13]

Give It Up

The next day, on Sunday, Serena Williams issued a written statement in which she admitted she had acted improperly, yet she still failed to make an apology.[14] Finally, on Monday, Williams issued another statement on her website. It included this apology: "I want to amend my press statement of yesterday, and want to make it as clear as possible—I want to sincerely apologize FIRST to the lineswoman, [then to opponent] Kim Clijsters, the USTA and tennis fans everywhere for my inappropriate outburst. I'm a woman of great pride, faith, and integrity, and I admit when I am wrong."[15] An apology shouldn't resemble a difficult dental extraction.

Grade: A

All of those botched apologies boosted criticism of and cut support for a parade of public figures. By way of contrast, let's review some examples of people and companies who made their apologies in a speedy, thoughtful, and complete way.

Career Save

He was driving a sparkling BMW and wore a baseball cap pulled low over his eyes. He flashed the car lights at her twice. She went into a side street to meet him.[16] When actor Hugh Grant decided to pay a prostitute for oral sex, he didn't think he would get stopped by police and put his career in jeopardy.

Grant quickly issued a statement: "Last night, I did something completely insane. . . . I am more sorry than I can ever possibly say."[17] On *The Tonight Show with Jay Leno* several nights later, he told his host, "I think you know in life what's a good thing to do and what's a bad thing, and I did a bad thing."[18] By admitting his mistake and apologizing, Grant saved his career. His box office successes since his evening in 1995 with Hollywood prostitute Divine Brown have included *Bridget Jones's Diary*, *About a Boy*, and *Love Actually*.

Sometimes Blue

In 2007, JetBlue airline stranded more than 100,000 passengers when bad weather crippled its ability to fly its planes. One flight remained on a snowed-in runway for more than nine hours. The JetBlue CEO apologized in a string of TV appearances and in full-page newspaper ads that said, "Words cannot express how truly sorry we are for the anxiety, frustration, and inconvenience that you, your family, friends, and colleagues experienced." Then he released a JetBlue Customer Bill of Rights that specifies what customers will receive when delays and cancellations occur. Within a week, JetBlue operations and ticket sales were back in gear.[19]

Grade: Incomplete

A grade of incomplete is rare for someone in public life because politicians, CEOs, and other high-level officials repeatedly have to explain and address various botches they commit or that occur under their leadership. But that wasn't the case for President George W. Bush. When asked in a 2004 presidential debate about mistakes he had made in his first term, the president responded that he could not name a single one.[20] Pitching a story of perfection won't sell. Apparently time and the absence of a forthcoming election have mellowed "W"; in his 2010 autobiography, *Decision Points*, he admits to some mistakes. Another famous incomplete: President Bill Clinton refused to use the words, "I am sorry" or "I apologize" after his untruthful grand jury testimony about his affair with Monica Lewinsky.

Instant Survivor™ Alert

What can we learn from these examples of good apologies, bungled apologies, and non-apologies about how and when to apologize in our own lives? The following rules can guide us.

MANAGER TIP #7—APOLOGIZE

If you have a colleague who is suffering a personal or professional crisis, ask him or her this question:

Is there someone you should think about apologizing to in a complete way immediately?

BE FIRST. If you do something wrong, you should be the first to admit it. Remember the Maryland judge who flattened a cleaning worker's tire? His supervisor found out about the incident when he read it in the local newspaper. When you do something wrong, immediately let the people in your life who shouldn't be caught off guard know about it.

BE FAST. Delay is a reputation killer. Serena Williams, Mel Gibson, and Tiger Woods soured their reputations by being slow to issue apologies. The clock starts ticking the moment an event occurs that requires an apology. Each tick of the clock hurts our reputations and shrinks our support.

MAKE IT PAST. In order to successfully put mistakes or wrongdoing behind us, we need to do three things in our apology:

- **Make it complete**. Mel Gibson had to apologize twice when his first effort did not address the anti-Semitic remarks at the heart of the controversy. When you apologize, make it a one-time event by making it complete.

- **Take action**. People hurt or offended by something we've said or done wonder what we are going to do about it, beyond making an apology. Taking action—meeting with the offended people, taking a course, getting professional help—makes your apology real by backing it up with action. If Serena Williams had wanted to galvanize her apology to the U.S. Open linesperson and fans, she would have announced she was taking an anger management course. Taking action helps reassure our supporters that we "get it" and won't do it again.

> **APOLOGIZE**
>
> It's hard to say, "My bad," but here's what you've got to do when you've made a mistake.
>
> - Be first.
> - Be fast.
> - Make it past.
>   ○ Make it complete.
>   ○ Take action.
>   ○ Move on.

- **Move on**. Our goal when we've done something wrong is to apologize, take action, and tie a snug knot around the issue or event and move on. Allow time to work. Don't obsess about your mistakes; we all make them. Apologize and move confidently into the future.

Why do apologies work? Making an apology signals strength. A recent study by professors at the University of Michigan and Stanford University demonstrates that companies that took responsibility for their poor financial performances had better stock prices than did companies that blamed others or external factors. The professors made this conclusion: shareholders reward companies that acknowledge their mistakes because shareholders believe those companies are in control of their businesses and able to make the changes necessary to improve performance.[21] Finally, we appreciate the courage it takes to apologize. We recognize the fact of life that we all goof up now and again and we appreciate that it's courageous to admit it.

•   •   •

Now you will not resist or struggle (or at least you'll do so a lot less) when you need to make an apology. You have the playbook. You will apologize quickly and completely, take constructive action, and move on.

You have completed the second step of *The Instant Survivor*™ System. Now you know how to secure support during a crisis by asking others for help, quickly taking decisive action, maintaining a high profile, and making an apology. All of these actions will solidify and broaden the support you need. Now it's time to move on to Step Three of the system: *stand tall.*

STEP
THREE

STAND TALL

How can we act like our heroes who handle disasters deftly?

Step Three offers the road map. Chapter eight explores why paper is so useful at this stage in a crisis: to identify what ails us, to evaluate options, and to revise our action plans. Chapter nine discusses how to be courageous in making sound decisions and not compounding mistakes. Chapter ten demonstrates why great crisis managers are flexible, and chapter eleven provides a formula for crafting messages to support your goals when you are in a mess.

PAPER WAS CREATED OVER FIVE THOUSAND YEARS AGO

In the first chapter of this book, we discussed how companies prepare a crisis management plan and how you can adopt that strategy to prepare a personal plan of your own. In addition to working from a written crisis management plan, companies keep a calendar log of events so they can judge how a disaster is unfolding. They draft further action plans that outline the company's strategy for managing particular issues created by the crisis. And they prepare "talking points" to use for various groups that want to understand what caused the upheaval and what's being done about it.

I have spent hours walking clients through this process. We always commit the details to paper to make sure that we stand tall and stay on task despite the distractions that a crisis throws our way. In order to become an *Instant Survivor*™, you too must sharpen your pencil and put your plans and talking points down on paper.

Did you know a piece of paper can even save your life? It did for Galen Litchfield. He was working for a Shanghai-based insurance company in World War II when the Japanese military invaded China. A Japanese admiral ordered the American to list all the insurance company's assets so they could be liquidated. Litchfield did so, yet he left off some securities owned by the company that were unrelated to the Shanghai business. When the admiral discovered this omission, he stormed around and announced that Litchfield was a thief and a traitor. The accusation of the furious Japanese admiral was enough to condemn the American to a Japanese torture house, where several of Litchfield's friends had died after days of torture. Litchfield, away from the office, heard about the admiral's tirade on a Sunday afternoon.

Litchfield immediately sat down and followed a lifelong habit. When worried, he took to his typewriter and typed out two questions: What am I worrying about? What can I do about it? This particular worry ranked higher than most; there was a good chance he could get thrown in the torture house. What could he do about it? He carefully examined and wrote out four options: try to explain (which risked upsetting the admiral again); try to escape (hopeless); not return to the office (would create suspicion); and go to the office as usual the next day (the admiral may have cooled down and, if not, Litchfield still would have a chance to explain). Litchfield followed the last option, and the admiral did not pursue the missing securities.

Litchfield told Dale Carnegie (quoted in *How to Stop Worrying and Start Living*): "I probably saved my life by sitting down that Sunday afternoon and writing out all the various steps I could take and then the probable consequence of each step and coming to a decision. If I hadn't done that, I might have floundered and hesitated and done the wrong thing on the spur of the moment."[1]

What does Litchfield have in common with Iraq war veterans, surgeons, and some homeless people? They, too, use paper to stand tall and save their lives or those of others.

Journal Your Way to Health

At the U.S. Army military base at Fort Bragg, North Carolina, soldiers in the Warrior Transition Battalion are working to get well so they can return to active duty or become civilians again. They suffer from post-traumatic stress disorder, and they are taking a class in therapeutic journaling. The class instructor, Michael J. Cain, a freelance writer and volunteer, finds journaling particularly useful for soldiers who struggle with trying to open up and express their feelings with psychiatrists and therapists. He ticks off the benefits he believes journaling provides for wounded veterans:

- "Soldiers can vent without fear of retribution, and clear their minds of stressful thoughts and memories."

- "Gives the ability to see one's thoughts from a new perspective . . . with a certain detachment, as if they belonged to another."

- "Helps to identify solutions that might not have been so obvious when they were just thoughts."[2]

Checklists Save Lives

Since 2001, intensive care unit doctors at Johns Hopkins Hospital in Baltimore have used a five-point checklist to eliminate central line infections. Use of the checklist prevented an estimated forty-three infections and eight deaths over a twenty-seven-month period.[3] Meanwhile, the same checklist used in Michigan decreased infections by two-thirds within three months and is estimated to have saved more than fifteen hundred lives within a year and a half.[4] By definition, every visit to the intensive care unit represents a crisis. In this dramatic setting, the crucially important surgical checklist highlights the value of putting points down on paper to avert further crises from developing.

Atul Gawande, author of *The Checklist Manifesto: How to Get Things Right*, concludes that doctors and pilots, who perform a huge volume of repetitive tasks, routinely overlook or omit steps in the many operations they perform daily.

The Homeless Compact

In Providence, Rhode Island, a group of around eighty homeless people live in tents under an abandoned overpass near the Providence River. What might appear to be a disorganized, ramshackle operation is anything but. The homeless community established a five-member leadership council. They also have a written compact that governs how they live together. It reads, in part, "No one person shall be greater than the will of the whole."

When two homeless men got into a drunken brawl, and one threatened the other with a knife taped to a stick, both were escorted from the community; they had violated the written compact. One was told not to return. His tent was taken down, his knife tossed into the river. The written compact helps keep order among often troubled homeless strangers; Rhode Island officials told *The New York Times* they had never seen anything like this homeless community.[5]

Instant Survivor™ Alert

How do we use paper in our lives? We often write down lists of various types, from grocery lists to wish lists. We write down To Do lists to prod ourselves and to nudge our forgetful teenagers and aging parents.

But do we write down our thoughts when it really matters? Remember that companies do this in a crisis to improve their decision-making because it helps remove emotion from the equation. Adapt this tool to help you become an *Instant Survivor*™ when facing a crisis.

If you have a colleague who is suffering a personal or professional crisis, ask him or her this question:

Have you written down your options, thought about keeping a journal, or drafted an action plan about this challenge?

Here are several ways you can use paper to help you navigate an upheaval in your life.

KEEP A JOURNAL. A journal can be an excellent way to gain insight into what's troubling you. Michael Cain, the therapeutic journaling teacher mentioned earlier, suggests trying it out for twenty minutes, once a week. After making a list of the things that cause you the most stress, identify the elements that contribute to your anxiety and possible solutions for them. Breaking a problem into pieces makes finding a solution easier. A journal also can simply serve as a coping tool to help you articulate your feelings and reactions to the events of the day or the week and find comfort in doing so.[6]

DRAFT AN ACTION PLAN. I explained earlier how to create an action plan as part of your personal crisis management plan. Just as Galen Litchfield responded to a crisis and created an action plan that saved his life, you must continuously update your action plan to address your changing situation. Here's a way to develop a mini-action plan that I've found useful, whether you've gotten a bad medical test result, you've lost your job, or you're facing a mountain of debt. Really, whatever it is, write down the answers to these four questions:

1. **In ten words or less, what is the problem?**

   By focusing on a short answer, it will really help you find a solution.

2. **Why do I have to get started on this problem right now?**

   This is such an important question. By answering the why question, you supply the motivation to get going on your problem.

3. **Who can help me?**

   The answer to this question is critical; there are so many people who want to help you and reach out to you in your time of trouble.

4. **What's the one step I can take right now to solve my problem?**

   Don't think about two, three, four, or five different things you can do. Just list one. Doing one thing will start up momentum toward solving your problem.

JOIN A CHAT ROOM. Some people enjoy the anonymity an online chat room provides. People who share your same concerns and are supportive to one another will populate a good one. Chat rooms can be great sources of encouragement; the participants typically don't offer advice and may not be equipped to do so.

START A BLOG. Consider writing a blog when a crisis arises. Unlike a journal, which typically is kept private, you may want to share your thoughts with others and, potentially, spark a dialogue that can illuminate ways to address your crisis.

Why is it so important to write down how you feel, then react and plan during a crisis? It will help you stand tall. You will be better informed, work more effectively and efficiently to address your problem, and avoid mistakes.

LEARN ABOUT THE SITUATION. You'll read in chapter seventeen how an injured reporter started writing down her reactions and impressions as soon as she woke up in the hospital. It helped her grasp what had happened to her and keep a sense of perspective. I recommend that anyone looking for a job keep a journal, because the combined opportunity to explore a new job and the pressure to find one creates swirling winds of hope and dread. By keeping a journal and looking back at it regularly, a job seeker finds that what made perfect sense just a few days ago may seem a lunatic idea today. A journal restores a sense of balance to a life threatening to go off the rails.

ESTABLISH GOALS AND TASKS. Effective goal-setting during a disaster requires putting them on paper. By listing goals together with the actions to take and the tasks to achieve them, we can emerge from the disorienting woods into a clear field.

PLANNING SAVES TIME. Time is your enemy in a crisis. Since any mess tends to get messier rather than cleaner over time, speeding up the cleanup process is valuable. Crisis situations tend to produce lots of thinking and too few decisions. Laying out your options on paper produces faster, better decisions.

PAPER WAS CREATED OVER FIVE THOUSAND YEARS AGO

Use paper to improve your life choices. Paper helps you

- Gain perspective on your situation.

- Identify goals, options, tasks, strategies.

- Save time.

- Lessen mistakes.

Write your thoughts out in a variety of ways:

- Option evaluation
- Journal
- Action plan
- Chat room
- Blog

AVOID MISTAKES UNDER PRESSURE. Airline pilots know they must keep calm during flight to survive. A misstep on a preflight checklist can down a plane. During the plummeting US Airways flight that landed in the Hudson River, the copilot, instructed by Captain Chesley Sullenberger, juggled one checklist for restarting the engine with another for how to ditch the plane. Checklists, studied by cool heads, saved the life of every passenger aboard Flight 1549.

Maximize your chance to stand tall by using paper to examine your options, gain perspective, and make sound decisions.

• • •

My clients always use paper as they evaluate strategies during a crisis, and so should you. The process of writing helps us to clarify the situation and make the kind of critical decisions that we will discuss in the next chapter.

SNOWBALLS ROLL DOWNHILL

You have to stand tall to make the right decisions. This is not easy. My corporate clients have to weigh a wide variety of interests as they consider their options in a crisis. They have to consider the interests of their employees, their shareholders, their customers, and numerous other stakeholders. Sometimes, there is tremendous pressure to make the wrong decision. It is hard to resist this pressure. I always advise my clients not to follow the easy path but to value long-term integrity over short-term benefits as they make their difficult decisions.

Move Past Pressure

Keysha Cooper was a senior mortgage underwriter at Washington Mutual ("WaMu"). Loan brokers and her supervisors squeezed her to approve loan applications. "At WaMu, it wasn't about the quality of the loans, it was about the number," Ms. Cooper told *The New York Times*. "They didn't care if we were giving loans to people that didn't qualify. Instead it was, 'How many loans did you guys close and fund?'" Cooper said loan officers who closed the most loans, whatever their quality, received vacation trips for a month to Hawaii and Jamaica.

Her supervisor criticized her for failing to approve one loan that Cooper felt certain was fraudulent. She was placed on probation for thirty days for refusing to sign off on the loan. Four months later the borrower defaulted after not making a single payment. WaMu supervisors wrote up Ms. Cooper several times for her insubordination in refusing to approve loans, and then she was laid off.[1] Federal regulators seized WaMu in September 2008, making it the biggest bank failure in the country's history.

* * *

Then there was the Enron scandal. Remember Sherry Watkins? She was the Enron employee who wrote a detailed seven-page letter to Ken Lay, the Enron CEO, where she laid out in blunt terms her concerns about the company. "I'm incredibly nervous that we will implode in a wave of accounting scandals," she wrote to Lay four months before the company filed for bankruptcy. "My eight years of Enron work history will be worth nothing on my resume, the business world will consider the past successes as nothing but an elaborate accounting hoax." She charged that accounting for certain Enron partnerships was "a bit like robbing the bank in one year and trying to pay it back two years later."[2] *Time* magazine named her one of its "People of the Year" in 2002.[3]

* * *

When we face our own personal crises, we need to stand as tall as Keysha Cooper and Sherry Watkins did. Suppose you are a man on a business trip away from home in a major city and meet a woman in a bar. You strike up a conversation and the woman suggests some work she can do for your company. You hire her and later begin an affair that produces a child. When rumors surface about your extramarital relationship, you deny it. Later, in the face of stronger evidence, you admit to the extended affair, but deny being the child's father. When asked to take a paternity test to determine whether the child is yours, you evade. Much later you admit you are the father. Your spouse, sick with cancer, files for divorce.

If the story sounds familiar, it is. The man is John Edwards, the former Democratic presidential candidate; his mistress is Rielle Hunter, a filmmaker hired to work for his presidential campaign; and Elizabeth Edwards was the spouse, who divorced him as she lay dying from cancer.[4]

The pathetic tale of John Edwards underscores why, to survive a crisis, we must have the fortitude to make difficult decisions under pressure. Edwards's crisis—an illicit affair—was his own fault, a self-inflicted gunshot wound. After his initial disastrous life decisions, Edwards faced two equally awful choices. Should he admit his wrongful conduct in full? Or should he deny involvement (and run the risk of later being forced to grudgingly admit the truth after his denials)? Edwards's choice of the second route exploded his marriage, strained his relationship with his children, and terminated any conceivable hope of future public service. Instead of standing tall, he shrank from a tough decision.

Stop

After we make a mistake, we must summon the strength not to worsen the situation. Of course the best approach, as President Teddy Roosevelt advised, is to make great decisions from the outset so we aren't trying to dig ourselves out from a mistake. But none of us throws a perfect game in life. So after you make a poor decision, stand tall and stop it. Don't make another one. Piling one poor decision on top of another only enables people to extend the crisis so they can hurtle past more caution signals and dash past more red flags until the inevitable: a spectacular crash.

Let's rewind the tape and see how poor decisions under pressure doomed any chance of a positive outcome to various crises and unnecessarily prolonged them.

The Sacred and the Profane

In the mid-1990s, the pedophilia scandal involving the Catholic Church broke wide open in the United States. The scandal had first been reported two decades earlier, when a Louisiana priest pleaded guilty to thirty-three counts of crimes against children and was imprisoned. Since then there have been thousands of similar cases, both civil and criminal, involving many thousands of children and billions of dollars in legal settlements.[5]

Let's count the ways the Catholic Church hierarchy stumbled in responding to the sex abuse scandal. Church leaders failed to ascertain the scope and magnitude of the problem both within the United States and worldwide. The church's policy of paying off victims suggested a cover-up. Church leaders became complicit in the problem by transferring abusive priests from one parish to another. They endorsed a psychological approach to the crisis, which enabled abusive priests to receive treatment and be returned to parishes (with disastrous results). Not until 2002 did the U.S. Conference of Catholic Bishops adopt a zero-tolerance policy that required reporting any priest who had sexually abused a minor to authorities and barring those priests from the ministry.[6]

Demonstrating a spectacular lack of judgment, the Vatican lashed out at critics of Pope Benedict XVI's involvement with the scandal, comparing them to anti-Semites.[7] How could the world's most sacred institution behave so profanely?

Throughout this tragic debacle, the Catholic Church created a crisis of confidence and a crisis of credibility. A church famous for protecting the vulnerable, for encouraging confession of sin, allowed its "shepherds" to abuse their most vulnerable "sheep," then refused to promptly confess to or address its own vast cache of sins. The irony is stunning. The widening scandal has recently led to the pope's own door, spawning questions about whether he himself had a hand in the unwise and most certainly unholy cover-up of the church's worldwide scandal.[8]

Who Is More of a Sinner?

Jasmine Co, a Catholic nurse living in Philadelphia, said she has turned to God directly rather than confessing to priests. "I don't believe in confession to the priest because I don't know if that priest is more of a sinner than I am," Co told the Associated Press.[9] According to a 2009 Pew Study, four American-born Catholics have left the church for every one new person who has converted to Catholicism since the 1960s.[10]

Through its inability to stand tall and make the right decisions, the Catholic Church prolonged its own scandal. This once-sacred authority on rules of Christian conduct exponentially multiplied the criticism it sparked by pursuing a profane course of out-of-step, secretive, and insensitive behavior.

Great Soldier, Poor Army

The Catholic Church is not the only trusted authority we count on that has recently brought shame upon itself by choosing a course of cover-up. Here is a sad story about the U.S. Army and a good military family it abused through dishonesty.

Nine months after the 9/11 attacks, pro football player Pat Tillman turned down an offer from the Arizona Cardinals of $3.6 million over three years to enlist in the army. Tillman's decision made him an instant American hero; for the army, it was a recruiting coup.

Tillman participated in the invasion of Iraq, then entered and graduated from Ranger School in Fort Benning, Georgia. He was deployed to Afghanistan. On April 22, 2004, the heroic former football star was killed. The army reported that Tillman and his unit were ambushed near the Pakistan border. The army further claimed that Tillman was killed by enemy fire.

A Continuing Cover-Up

Within days of the shooting, U.S. Army officials learned a very different version of the story, however. They concluded that Tillman was likely killed by friendly fire when one group of American soldiers fired on another after mistakenly deciding that nearby gunfire was coming from the enemy. Even though the high-ranking officers knew the truth about how Tillman actually died, the army persisted in awarding him the Silver Star, weaving a detailed account of his death "in the line of devastating enemy fire."

The cover-up continued. The military ordered Tillman's fellow soldiers to lie to his family at the funeral. At a nationally televised memorial service, Tillman was described as a war hero who died fighting the enemy.

It wasn't until weeks after his memorial service that army spokesmen confessed to Tillman's family that this dedicated soldier was actually killed by friendly fire. Tillman's brother, Kevin, who enlisted in the U.S. Army on the same day as Pat, later testified, "We have been used as props in a Pentagon public relations exercise." Pete Geren, then acting secretary of the army, said later, "We as an Army failed in our duty to the Tillman family, the duty we owe to all the families of our fallen soldiers: *give them the truth, the best as we know it, as fast as we can* [emphasis added]."[11] While the army stacked one poor decision on top of another once it chose to lie about Tillman's death, at least Secretary Geren provides a model for how we should conduct ourselves when called to account for what we've said or done.

Slow-Walk

Remember when U.S. Vice President Dick Cheney shot a fellow quail hunter on a Texas ranch on February 11, 2006? Cheney's decision to slow-walk the report of the shooting and his failure to apologize to his injured friend sparked a media feeding frenzy and an explosion of jokes, and it led to a further decline in Cheney's already low poll ratings.

Although the accident occurred on a Saturday afternoon, it was first reported on Sunday by the ranch owner who called in news of the incident to a local Texas newspaper. That same afternoon, the Bush administration disclosed the shooting incident. On Monday night, February 13, comedian David Letterman began his show: "Good news, ladies and gentlemen. We have finally located weapons of mass destruction . . . it's Dick Cheney." Jon Stewart of *The Daily Show* teased, "Cheney's got a gun," playing off the Aerosmith song titled "Janie's Got a Gun."

Meanwhile, Cheney ignored the gathering media storm. He avoided reporters by leaving early from an Oval Office meeting with UN Secretary-General Kofi Annan and waited until February 15, four days after the accident, to appear on the Fox News Channel, where he finally accepted full responsibility for the accident.

When the victim, Harry Whittington, was discharged from the hospital on February 17, 2006, he graciously told a press conference: "My family and I are deeply sorry for everything Vice President Cheney and his family have had to deal with. We hope that he will continue to come to Texas and seek the relaxation that he deserves."[12] In a 2010 interview, Whittington did not dispute that he never received an apology from Dick Cheney.[13]

Despite these distressing examples of compounded mistakes, let's remember the brave citizens who have made the tough decision to stand tall in the face of government wrongdoing during the last decade.

Who Am I to Do That?

You've probably never heard of Thomas M. Tamm. He worked in the Justice Department in the George W. Bush administration and had a security clearance at a level above Top Secret. He worked in a unit that handled wiretaps of suspected terrorists and spies; to enter the unit he had to place his hand through a biometric scanner. Tamm learned about a highly classified National Security Agency program that eavesdropped on U.S. citizens without the required approval of a panel of federal judges.

Tamm struggled about what to do before he finally tipped off *The New York Times*. The newspaper broke a front-page story that President Bush had secretly authorized the spy agency to intercept the calls and e-mail of American citizens without judicial approval, as required.

The FBI opened a criminal investigation and Tamm quickly became a target. His wife, children, and neighbors got the third degree. Tamm is chastened by the results of his decision. "I didn't think through what this could do to my family," he told *Newsweek* magazine. Nevertheless, he stands by his whistle-blowing. "I thought this was something the other branches of the government—and the public—ought to know about. So they could decide: Do they want this massive spying program to be taking place?" Tamm, who spoke to *Newsweek* against the advice of his lawyers, concluded, "If somebody were to say, who am I to do that? I would say, 'I have taken an oath to uphold the Constitution.'"[14]

•   •   •

The courage of Keysha Cooper, Sherry Watkins, and Thomas Tamm won national attention, but the predicament each one of them faced—namely, being called upon to make challenging decisions under pressure—is a daily reality.

Instant Survivor™ Alert

Note: It's very likely that because of something we say or do at work or in our personal lives we will be compelled to make difficult decisions under pressure. How can we muster the courage to refuse to participate in illegal or unethical activity, admit when we've said or done something wrong, or resist compounding an already bad decision?

MANAGER TIP #9—SNOWBALLS ROLL DOWNHILL

If you have a colleague who is suffering a personal or professional crisis, ask him or her this question:

Have you thought about what decision you must make in this situation? Will you look back proudly on that decision?

Suggestion: Think back to our discussion in chapter eight about using paper to map out options. Use that technique when you're under pressure to make a decision you don't feel comfortable about. Ask yourself this series of questions and actually write down your candid, no-stone-unturned answer to each one:

How will this crisis unfold?
How could this situation get worse?
How will I look if the truth comes out?
What do I stand for?
What values do I uphold?
What should I say or do so I can hold my head high for myself, my
    family, my friends, my organization, and my country?

SNOWBALLS ROLL DOWNHILL

- Life will require you to make difficult decisions under pressure.
- Analyze the impact of your decisions on yourself, others, and your reputation.
- If you make a bad decision, stop—don't pile another one on top of it.

Honest answers to these questions will prompt you to stand tall under stress.

. . .

Part of making a tough business decision is that you must hold tightly to your convictions in the face of strong opposition and personal sacrifice. Standing tall means keeping your backbone strong and straight, but it also requires a great deal of flexibility, as we will learn in the next chapter.

THE FLEXIBLE ARE FAVORED

"Government's trial and error helped stem financial panic," blared a 2009 front-page *Wall Street Journal* headline. While there is no final verdict on the performance of the U.S. Treasury and the U.S. Federal Reserve in addressing the 2008 financial collapse, it appears that they should get high marks for employing a variety of techniques, freely changing their mind when necessary, and ultimately preserving our financial system. "It was a period of tremendous experimentation," says Columbia University economist Frederic Mishkin, who left the Fed board in August 2008. "When you're faced with a crisis of this magnitude, if you take the view that every measure that we take has to be exactly right, you don't do anything."[1]

When an explosion killed eight and injured several more people on the West Coast, the local utility that thought it might be responsible wanted to act quickly to help the families of the deceased and others harmed by the explosion.

Their problem: no access to quick cash within the company. Because the utility is government regulated, check approval was a slow, cumbersome process that often took weeks. The solution? The human resources chief of staff stepped in and personally bought $20,000 of gift cards to hand out to survivors. His flexible approach helped enhance the company's reputation with its customers. And yes, he did get reimbursed!

As crises unfold for my clients, it is my job as an advisor to provide new perspectives that will allow companies and individuals to flexibly shift strategies as circumstances are changing. Maintaining this kind of flexibility, however, is as difficult for an individual as it is for a large organization when it locks in to crisis mode.

"Successful Failure"

After an explosion in the *Apollo 13* spacecraft cut oxygen and power to the command module, astronaut Jack Swigert famously advised NASA, "Houston, we've had a problem here."[2] Gene Kranz, lead flight director for Houston Mission Control, quickly shifted the mission's goal from landing on the Moon to returning to Earth. "Forget the flight plan," Kranz ordered the ground crew. "From this moment on we are improvising a new mission. How do we get our men home?"

Even though Kranz announced that "failure was not an option," he knew the challenge was steep.[3] Would there be enough power for the return trip from 200,000 miles away? NASA turned off all noncritical systems in the spacecraft and reduced energy consumption to a fifth of the usual level. The temperature dropped to 38 degrees. Water was in short supply; the crew cut their intake to six ounces per day. While there was enough oxygen for astronauts Swigert, Jim Lovell, and Fred Haise, carbon dioxide was the major threat. If they couldn't successfully remove the toxic gas they were exhaling, they would die. NASA walked the astronauts step by step through building an air scrubber using cardboard, a plastic cover from a flight plan, a spacesuit hose, and a sock.[4] Cool heads and recalculations saved the day.

After the astronauts arrived home safely, NASA dubbed their mission a "successful failure." While the original mission to land on the

Moon had not been achieved, the rescue of the astronauts was hailed as a resounding success.

. . .

This brings to mind another historical example of the importance of flexibility when it matters most—in this case, when America's future hung in the balance.

U.S. soldiers landing on the Normandy beaches on D-day during World War II quickly found themselves pinned down below rugged hills facing fierce machine-gun fire. They got separated from their units; their senior officers were killed. Groups of army soldiers—strangers to each other but similarly trained—pulled together to successfully assault the Nazi fortresses at the top of the hills. The fabled D-day owes its very success to the U.S. Marines' approach to war: accept and embrace its uncertainty, adapt, adjust, and be flexible.[5]

"Surgical Strike"

Let's go back once more, this time to October 1962. When President John F. Kennedy learned that the Soviet Union was installing nuclear missiles in Cuba, ninety miles away from U.S. soil, many advisors pushed him to blow up the missiles. While the military promised a "surgical strike," Kennedy knew that initiating an attack on Cuba could prompt the Soviet Union to launch nuclear missiles against the States.

What did he do? Kennedy established a blockade around Cuba to stop any additional shipments arriving from the Soviet Union and then quietly negotiated a trade in which the Soviets would remove their missiles from Cuba provided the United States removed its missiles in Turkey. Catastrophe averted.

. . .

NASA's flexibility in handling the *Apollo 13* crisis, the flexibility of our troops during D-day, and Kennedy's flexibility as he faced down the Soviets in Cuba highlight our own need to be flexible in handling the big and small challenges we face during a crisis. Why is it so critical for us to adjust and adapt as events unfold and demand change?

OUR INITIAL APPROACH MAY HAVE BEEN WRONG. Nobel Prize winner Martin Chalfie told *Science News*, "I would say that a good 95 percent—maybe I'm being generous to myself—of my ideas turn out to be wrong. We make mistakes all the time."[6] Progress in science depends on conducting experiments to test a hypothesis, and those experiments often fail before they produce groundbreaking approaches. While we hope that we aren't wrong in our approach to life 95 percent or more of the time, we must be willing to abandon poor ideas.

"TRY SOMETHING." Let's examine the spectrum of flexibility demonstrated by certain U.S. presidents. In a *Rolling Stone* magazine article in 2006, Princeton professor and presidential historian Sean Wilentz highlighted President George W. Bush's characteristic inflexibility: "[He] has also displayed a weakness common among the greatest presidential failures—an unswerving adherence to a simplistic ideology that adjures deviation from dogma as heresy, thus preventing a pragmatic adjustment to changing realities."[7] By contrast, Wilentz places Franklin D. Roosevelt, who led the country through the Great Depression and World War II, in the top rank of presidents, including Washington and Lincoln, whose successes stemmed from their ability to adjust as events demanded.[8] President Roosevelt summed up his plan for our nation to escape the Depression: "The country demands bold, persistent experimentation. It is common sense to take a method and try it; if it fails, admit it frankly and try another. *But above all, try something.*"[9]

AN ENTIRELY DIFFERENT APPROACH IS REQUIRED. One of the harsh lessons from the recent economic downturn: highly paid employees may have to start over. Chad Smith skipped college because he landed high-paying construction and auto industry jobs. "When you're making $55,000 at eighteen years old," Smith told the *Wall Street Journal*, "it's hard to tell yourself to go to school." After being laid off from his night shift job at Chrysler, Smith found himself back in school at twenty-nine years old, studying software development and computer networking.[10]

THE INITIAL APPROACH MAY HAVE BEEN RIGHT, BUT CIRCUM-STANCES HAVE WORSENED. In war zones, soldiers face life-threatening choices. They start out on patrol, for example, and walk into an ambush. Their initial approach may have been right, but circumstances have worsened for them, dramatically.

Few of us will face such a harrowing choice. Yet we realize that our most pressing challenges and most threatening "issues" tend to worsen over time and, consequently, may require new, bold approaches.

On a lighter note (because, believe me, I want you to stay with me), let me tell you about comedian Groucho Marx's philosophy on being flexible: "These are my principles: if you don't like them I have others."[11] In fact, while we should maintain our principles under pressure, we should likewise eagerly adjust our tactics, techniques, and goals as needed.

Instant Survivor™ Alert

How can you stand tall and be flexible during a personal or professional crisis? Here are concrete steps you can set in place so that you're ready whenever, as the omnipresent bumper sticker warns, "S**t happens."

MANAGER TIP #10—THE FLEXIBLE ARE FAVORED

If you have a colleague who is suffering a personal or professional crisis, ask him or her this question:

Have you considered a different way of approaching this challenge?

Get ready now. Start assessing yourself. Are you unyielding in your views at work and at home? Once you make a decision to follow a certain path, do you stay on it no matter how it is working? Do your friends and family tease you about being stubborn? Start to work on becoming more flexible in your approach to life; you will adapt more easily to change, the constant in any crisis. Remember Charles Darwin's admonition: *"It is not the strongest of the species that survive. It is the one that is most adaptable to change."* He didn't invent the idea; he merely documented its success through all time.

Monitor your progress. When Ed Koch was mayor of New York City, he would shout out to residents in the Big Apple, "How'm I doing?" What a great question to ask ourselves during an upheaval. Have you seen a nature movie that shows a tiger moving in on its prey? The tiger is constantly evaluating its position and adjusting to its prey's movement, until it is ready to strike. Be self-aware, take down your blinders, have your receptors up, and react to change.

Search for multiple solutions. When a mine collapsed in Chile in 2010 and trapped thirty-three miners, Chile's president took over the rescue effort. He mobilized help from around the world and launched three separate efforts to rescue the workers. What is your plan B? Your plan C? Can your crisis be solved by any one of several approaches? If so, start exploring them simultaneously.

．　．　．

Standing tall while remaining flexible allows companies to incorporate new strategies as they grapple with challenging crises. Standing tall also means remaining visible to the public. Such visibility requires companies to explain their strategies with effective messaging. As an individual, you may not need a high-powered public relations firm; you yourself will have to develop clear messages, as we'll discuss in the next chapter.

THE FLEXIBLE ARE FAVORED

Flexible people find solutions.

- The initial effort may not work.
- An entirely different approach may be required.
- Changed circumstances may demand adaptation.

Be flexible during a crisis.

- Focus yourself to be more flexible in your life.
- Monitor your progress in solving a crisis.
- Search for multiple solutions from the outset.

IT'S THE MESSAGE, STUPID

When I was a young lawyer I helped defend a government employee accused of padding his expense account. He was near the end of an honorable career. Numerous magazine articles lauded his skillful handling of critical missions. Although in many ways a hero, my client pleaded guilty. My job: make sure he didn't go to jail. As it turns out, my job was a fairly standard communications assignment: send short, simple, and strong messages to the sentencing judge.

What were the messages I needed to communicate? First, a small amount of money was involved. Second, why send a patriot to jail when it would only sour morale in his department? Third, instead of jail, why not require him to perform extensive community service? The judge wrestled with whether to give him the prison term the prosecutors wanted, but ultimately decided on probation and sent him home to his family.

What Do You Want to Say?

As we've discussed, a crisis in your world puts you in the spotlight. You know that you need to keep your wits about you, get help, and make difficult decisions under pressure. You appreciate how important it is to stay visible to your allies so that they see you are not beaten down, distressed, or depressed by the upheaval in your life. Let's talk now about what you want to say to friends, acquaintances, and others about how you're responding to what you're going through. You must send a message that you are standing tall despite your disaster.

Imagine you learn that a friend is in trouble. At the end of a conversation with your friend, you will evaluate how he or she is bearing up. Is your friend taking charge of the situation/crisis and does she or he have a plan to improve it and move on? As we've discussed, we are more likely to help people who are helping themselves—by being calm, thoughtful, and active.

More important, are you sending that message—be calm, thoughtful, and active—to *yourself* when you are in trouble?

Here's a little reality check. The first problem we face when sending our message out is the clutter of other messages that fill up our lives—from TV, radio, the Internet, strangers, friends, and family. "Breaking through" that clutter isn't just a challenge for Madison Avenue advertisers, it's a challenge for us. Advertisers catch our attention with short, punchy slogans: "Just do it" (Nike), "Where's the beef?" (Wendy's), "We try harder" (Avis). Great presidencies, Peggy Noonan wrote in the *Wall Street Journal*, can be told in a single sentence. She pointed out that sometimes you don't even have to hear a president's name to know who is being referred to. "He preserved the Union and freed the slaves" (Lincoln) or "He lifted us out of a great depression and helped to win a World War" (Franklin Roosevelt).[1] If she summarized Ronald Reagan's presidency, it might be, "He ended the Cold War." Although you may not need to condense your messages to such politically expedient minibites, make sure they are nonetheless memorable.

Divide the Page in Half

Journalists and public relations specialists both routinley divide a piece of paper in half to do their work. Reporters will write the questions they plan to ask on the left side of the page and then fill in the interviewee's responses on the right side. Meanwhile, PR specialists will predict what questions the media will ask their clients and write them down on the left side of the page and then use the right side to draft proposed responses to the questions.[2]

Companies in crisis work with their legal and public relations advisors to craft messages for the "right side of the page" that are truthful, reassuring, and easy for everyone from the media to employees to remember and repeat. The questions the public wants answered in any crisis are these: "What happened?" "Why?" "Who is to blame?" and "What are you doing about it?"

Let's see how this approach applies in our lives. If you lose your job, think how your relatives, friends, allies, and others will divide the page in thinking about you. The left-hand side of the page may end up with a series of "mixed" bullet points, such as "Hope she's doing okay"; "He got laid off"; "She's a loser"; "He's really screwed"; "Wow, isn't that too bad." Your job is to tilt perceptions in your favor by filling in the empty right-hand half of the page in a way that reassures your supporters and potential allies that you are standing tall. Think about some upbeat messages it would make sense to send them: "I'm doing fine," "Good time to reinvent myself," or "This is giving me a chance to regroup."

Instant Survivor™ Alert

So let's go ahead and pretend you have lost your job. What messages do you want to send now? How many messages do you want to send? How long should those messages be? Companies in crisis have adopted certain ground rules for developing messages that have stood the test of time.

- First, your messages should follow the "3S" rule: *short, simple, strong.*

- Second, provide no more than three messages.

- Third, each message should contain no more than nine words.[3]

Imagine you are recently unemployed and you run into a friend at the grocery store who says quietly, "Sorry to hear you lost your job." What do you say? What is your elevator pitch (meaning what you would say to him or her in an elevator ride of about thirty seconds)? What are the sound bites you want to send? What do you want this person's take-away to be about you and your situation? When we react emotionally, without a strategy, we can fall into complainer/loser mode and tell our friend: "It's really unfair. My boss hated me. Don't know what I'm going to do now." Even a nonchalant response such as, "No worries, it'll be fine," can be counterproductive by suggesting that you're unrealistic or uninterested in help.

MANAGER TIP #11—IT'S THE MESSAGE, STUPID

If you have a colleague who is suffering a personal or professional crisis, ask him or her this question:

What message do you want to send about your situation to your allies—and how can you make it short, simple, and strong?

Let's craft three messages, no more than nine words each, that will highlight you as a thoughtful, upbeat, and resourceful person.

MESSAGE ONE: *"Thanks—I really appreciate your interest."* This message shows you are taking the situation in stride and are thinking about people other than yourself. You should try to avoid answering the unspoken "why did it happen?" and "who's to blame?" questions; doing so will probably end the discussion in a bad place. Instead, you want to focus the conversation on your future.

MESSAGE TWO: *"I've made some networking calls already."* This message says that you are taking charge, that you're upbeat and not scared.

MESSAGE THREE: *"I'd like your help in expanding my search."* This request shows confidence and a focus on getting a new job. The open-ended nature of your request will likely spark a question from your friend, which you can answer more specifically and should produce assistance.

When companies face a crisis, they tend to get fixated on what they'll say to the media. I tell them to think "do" before "say," meaning that figuring out what to do matters more and will furnish the right message. That's true for you as well when trouble strikes. Follow your plan, figure out what to do, and then develop short, simple, and strong messages that support your plan and image of standing tall.

* * *

As we maintain our visibility in a crisis and make the tough decisions, we have to take care to communicate what we are doing to those around us. Entire industries are based on helping companies produce the appropriate message. You may have to craft your own message, but if you do it effectively you will succeed in standing tall.

> **IT'S THE MESSAGE, STUPID**
>
> Silence is not an option.
>
> - Send short, simple, strong messages.
> - Provide no more than three messages.
> - Each message should have no more than nine words.

In Step Three of the personal crisis management system you have learned to stand tall by writing down your new strategies, making sound decisions that don't compound mistakes, remaining flexible, and delivering effective messages. You must remain standing tall until your crisis has passed. Now you've reached the point where it is time to save your future.

STEP
FOUR

SAVE YOUR FUTURE

Once a company has survived a crisis, it doesn't stop working on crisis management. In fact, it's just the opposite. Sharp companies model their actions after the U.S. Army, which conducts reviews after every combat action during a war. In the After-Action Report, troops involved in the action assess how to build on their strengths and improve their weaknesses so they will fight better in the next battle.

An After-Action Report is the third essential section of any crisis management plan. (Diagnosis and Action are the first and second ones, as you'll recall.) It provides companies with the guidance they need to look ahead and save their futures.

In the following section, you will see how to look beyond the current crisis and prepare yourself for the next crisis, which, inevitably, you will have to face. Chapter twelve rallies you to accept that your future will be different when the crisis is over, but it can be equally bright, if not brighter. In chapter thirteen, we'll look at the importance of preparing for "soft" crises such as personal or career setbacks, which may be even more difficult to survive than "hard" crises such as accidents or robberies.

Chapter fourteen will help you define who you are and what you want to be as you move through a crisis, while chapters fifteen and sixteen take you through a personal threat assessment process similar to those used by the most successful companies. Finally, chapter seventeen gets back to the basics—the importance of training to prepare for any crisis in the future.

So, keep your eyes on the horizon as you learn how to save your future as an *Instant Survivor*™.

YOUR FUTURE IS YOUR FRIEND

As the members of a corporate team reach the end of a crisis, they are exhausted. They have spent long hours under terrific pressure, striving to stay frosty, secure support, and stand tall. As their energy drains away, some of them begin to dread the future and the inevitable crises it will bring. I encourage my clients to put the past behind them and look positively toward the future. Adopting a proper attitude gives companies and individuals the strength they need to view the future as their friend.

The Greatest Hurdler of All Time

In the spring of 2010, Danny Harris seemed just like many other college seniors. He struggled with math. He was interested in sports and worked as a volunteer coach for the track team. He wondered about what job he could get after graduation.

But Danny is different. He's forty-four years old. He's married. He was an Olympic silver medalist and world-class track star twenty-five years ago, and the path that led him back to college was long and incredibly arduous.

Danny grew up in Compton, California, near South Central Los Angeles, the youngest of six children. His father died in a car accident when Danny was three years old. His mother had a stroke and died when he was fourteen. He told *Runner's World* magazine, "I wasn't a boy, but I wasn't a man either. I felt like I was on an island by myself."[1] Orphaned, he then lived with his grandmother. During the summers, he and his grandmother would get up at 4:30 a.m. to cut onions with migrant workers so she could avoid going on welfare. When I talked to Danny, he told me his work ethic of being able to stay out a little bit longer, do a little bit more, and be a little more driven started with a grandmother who was willing to get up and do what she did when she was in her sixties.

He was a track star in high school and was recruited to run at Iowa State. After his freshman year, he won a silver medal in the 400-meter hurdles in the 1984 Los Angeles Olympics. He went on to win three national championships and have an undefeated record as a collegiate hurdler. He told me he thought he would make a million dollars, run in four Olympic Games, and retire as the greatest 400-meter hurdler of all time.

In a 1987 international race, Danny broke the 121-race winning streak of 1984 gold medal winner Edwin Moses. Danny appeared ready to challenge Moses for dominance in the hurdles. As Danny was preparing for the 1988 Olympic Trials, he pulled a hamstring. He still ran a fast time (one that would have won him a silver medal at the 2008 Olympics),[2] but four other Americans finished ahead of him at the trials in what he called "the American golden age of 400-meter hurdles when five of the top ten people in the world were Americans, but only three can make the Olympic team."

"Addicted the very first time I tried it."

After the trials, Danny returned to Ames, Iowa, deeply disappointed, with nothing to do. Instead of being on his way to the Olympics in

Seoul, South Korea, he was alone in a college town that was out for summer. He had been a pot smoker and occasional heavy drinker since his mother's death, and one night he freebased cocaine.[3] Danny told me, "I think I was addicted the very first time I tried it." He said that because he was so afraid of being caught, he became totally isolated when he got hooked on drugs; he swiftly crossed the line from casual drug user to addict. Removed from friends and family, he had no one to tell him to slow down or to provide checks or controls on what he was doing.

Danny started getting ready for the 1992 Olympic Games. He was able to smoke crack, keep it a secret, and run great times. But he tested positive for cocaine in the spring of 1992 and was suspended for four years. "I wasn't speaking to anyone because no one knew what I was doing and I had totally isolated myself from everyone. Had it not been for the fact that I failed the drug test, I don't think any of my friends or my coach would have been aware of what was actually going on with me, which is why I think it took some people by shock . . . because I was a private person and I stayed in a private place."

No secret anymore. Danny did a couple of stints in rehab, first for thirty days, and then for six months.

Danny said he felt like he'd had a major setback, but even though he realized cleaning himself up from drugs wasn't going to be easy, he didn't think his career was over. "I had some work to do to restore my image as well as live life. Not fully accepting the fact that I was an addict made it tougher, because then I'm trying to live in two different worlds, and that doesn't work. I thought I would be able to bounce back and go forward." His rehab efforts failed. Danny resumed using cocaine.

With the help of his college coach, Danny applied for and received an early reinstatement and started to get ready for the 1996 Olympic Trials. Then he tested positive again. He was banned from running, for life.[4] No Olympics, yet again.

A Bouncing Ball

Danny accepted that he wouldn't be able to run again:

> It was a relief in some ways, because then the responsibility
> wasn't there to be Danny Harris the runner. I just needed to be
> Danny Harris the person. . . . Trying to extricate myself from
> the runner to be the regular guy who was going to get a job and
> live a regular life was a lot harder than I thought it was going to
> be.

After his suspension, Danny said he immersed himself in drugs and
alcohol before pursuing recovery in a real way. He started rehab, came
out clean, relapsed, returned to rehab, and moved in and out of various jobs, support groups, and crack dens. He lost touch with his family. Then he was diagnosed with colon cancer. After his chemotherapy
treatment, he left Des Moines and went back to Los Angeles to live
with his sister.

Once he recovered from cancer, he got a job at a private gym. He
was on his way there on his bike one morning at 5:30 a.m. when police
pulled up, threw him on the ground, arrested him, and charged him
with kidnapping, burglary, and auto theft. Bail was set at $1.4 million.
He was put in a Los Angeles County jail cell built for four men that
housed six. Danny describes, "My grandmother used to say that God
never gives you more than you can handle. But on those days when
they're taking me to court, I'm handcuffed to twenty other guys, and
I'm riding the bus down the freeway . . . and they're talking about life
plus sixteen years, sometimes that gets a little bit rough." Ultimately,
the police found the true kidnapper and released Danny after he'd
spent two and a half months in jail. The police never apologized, and
Danny emerged extremely angry. He had lost his job, his apartment,
and everything he owned.

"The best year of my life."

Before being jailed, Danny had been sober for eleven months, but he ended up back on drugs and back in rehab. Sometimes he lived on the streets, sometimes in shelters. Finally, in 2005, he stayed in a treatment center for a year. He recognized that during his earlier rehab efforts, he had resisted changing and listening to and helping others. "I finally took a time-out and wasn't willing to go out and try to do things on my own. I took suggestions from people who had time in the program . . . from people who I trusted . . . from people I didn't like when I was sober, because I wanted to be sober." It was also a year of service because he cooked meals for guys in the house and escorted people to doctors' appointments. He called it "probably the best year of my life."

Finally clean, Danny Harris met his wife. They were married on New Year's Eve 2009 in Ames, Iowa, with his Iowa State track coach and his wife in attendance. Danny's wife agreed that he could return to Iowa State University to try to earn the sixteen credits he was missing and graduate. He earned a 3.6 average and now aims to be a Division One college track and field coach. He helps teenagers at a nearby substance abuse center.

Danny survived—and has since thrived—because of tremendous faith and determination. He is philosophical about the ups and downs of his life.

> Had I not gone through everything I've gone through, I wouldn't be here talking to you now . . . as long as I continue to do the things I've done every day, I think I can stay in this state of happiness and freedom . . . I hope to be able to show others how they can do it as well. . . . Sometimes we need to get out of situations that are toxic for us. That can be relationships, it can be jobs, it can be anything. . . . If a person can go through what I've been through and come out on the other side, then I think that anything is possible.

Danny learned to believe in the future through his roller-coaster life. Let's look at some other ways that people make their future their friend in the face of disability, violence, disaster, and death. How do they stay frosty, secure support, and stand tall despite their challenges?

Use Calamity for Clarity

The economic turbulence during the last several years has meant career calamity for millions of Americans. Lee Child, a TV and movie producer, worked his entire career for one company until it bounced him out at age thirty-nine in a round of layoffs. He wrote in a *Parade* magazine article that initially he was upset and frustrated. He felt betrayed by his own naïveté because the world had changed and he "hadn't seen it coming." Most of all, he felt scared because his finances had no margin and the jobs that he would want to do were elusive.

But Lee masked his anger, fear, and frustration; he asked himself how he could be his own boss in the entertainment world. He decided that his firing was about opportunity, not just loss. He identified his dream, believed in himself, and became a best-selling thriller writer. He urges laid-off employees to take the chance to figure out what they really want, because one's "motivation will never be as strong" as at that moment, "and the chance might never come your way again."[5] Lee asked a question that smart companies pursue during a crisis: "Where do we want to be when it's over?"

David Koller had a similar experience. He was a young lawyer who got laid off two years ago by his Philadelphia law firm. He wrote in *The Legal Intelligencer* that he actually didn't feel that bad about it and took the opportunity to ask himself these questions: "Was the job what I really wanted? Was I happy? Did I see a long future for myself working in the traditional law firm environment?" Once he got home, he said it really only took a walk with his two dogs for him to decide to open up his own law firm.[6]

My friend Jim Hanks is a Baltimore lawyer who had the misfortune of being on the notorious US Airways flight that landed in the Hudson River on January 15, 2009. Seated in the back of the plane, Jim headed for the nearest exit, only to find the door twisted, bent, and jammed. The water pouring into the plane rose up to his neck. He assumed he would drown. He didn't see how he was going to reach a forward exit before the water was over his head. Fortunately, as others moved forward, the plane's nose tipped down and the water receded. Jim made it out alive.

The next day he went out to the airport to take a flight to Charlotte. His thinking was simple, he told the *Maryland Bar Bulletin*: "I can't let my life be run by a bunch of geese."[7] Hanks is an international lawyer who travels a lot throughout the year. He emerged from the plane wreck not only alive but also full of focus and resilience.

Give Meaning to Disaster

At age sixteen, Pakistan native Assiya Rafiq was kidnapped, and for a year thereafter, she was raped and beaten by thugs. When she was finally delivered to the police, four police officers took turns raping her. The expected response was for her to commit suicide, which is the cultural standard in rural Pakistan as the only way a rape victim can cleanse the disgrace to her family.

But Assiya, despite threats against her and her sisters, is seeking to prosecute both the thugs who kidnapped her and the police. "I decided to prosecute because I don't want the same thing to happen to anybody else," she told *The New York Times*.[8] A survivor of unthinkable brutalities, this brave woman has dedicated her life to a mission to protect others from suffering similar atrocities.

A drive to help others motivated yet another young woman facing a severe challenge, a medical nightmare.

Sometimes a person's body can be her own worst enemy. Kristen Shovlin is allergic to gluten, a protein found in wheat, rye, and barley. Unfortunately, she didn't know it and neither did eleven different specialists she visited over a six-year period. "I suffered from fatigue, anemia, abdominal discomfort, weight loss, and back pain. I just got sicker and sicker," she told the *Hudson Hub Times*.[9] When she was finally diagnosed with celiac disease, she was able to resume her work in the medical field. Now she's started her own business, Celiac Made Simple, which helps those with the disease live healthier lives through education and personal counseling.

Keith Buckman was also once a victim. He narrowly survived a suicide bombing in Iraq that killed three fellow Marines and left him with both his legs and one arm shattered. But one year later, he was training for the Paralympic Games. In the spring of 2008, the U.S. Olympic Committee launched a paralympic military program to identify promising disabled veterans or soldiers and offer them coaching and other resources. Buckman, who grew up playing football, basketball, and soccer, told the *Washington Post*: "Doing sports makes me feel normal again."[10] Besides being more "normal," he serves as an inspirational role model to other injured athletes.

Put Your Past in Perspective

Warren Morris played baseball for LSU. In the deciding game of the 1996 College World Series, his team trailed by a run, with a runner on third and two men out, when he came up to bat in the final inning. Before he came to bat, Morris had decided that he was going to be aggressive. "If I strike out, I strike out. But I'm going out swinging," Morris told the *American Banker* newspaper. Morris hit a two-run home run to win the game. He believes that sports are a good metaphor for many life lessons. "In anything you do, be prepared to succeed," he said. "And remember, the sun comes up every day. So even if you strike out today, that will only affect you tomorrow if you don't let it go."[11]

Investments are another realm of life that requires us to take risks to avoid being controlled by our past decisions. Securities firm president Scott Koonce knows that investing isn't just a financial art; it's an emotional one as well. He says his clients are often too focused on the price of a stock when they bought it, which they let influence their decision on whether to sell or hold it. Koonce told *Washington Business Journal*: "People need to concentrate on the company and what its prospects are going forward. How strong are its earnings prospects? How safe are its dividends? People should think about these sorts of things rather than making snap decisions based on how much they've gained or lost on a particular security."[12]

Think how Koonce's investing approach can help us in our lives. Wherever you are, whatever you've done, whatever you've suffered, make your investment in yourself and your future based on your analysis of your future prospects—not because of where you have been, what you have done, and what has happened to you.

Imagine being laid off from one job, finding another one, and being laid off again. All within four months. That happened to Inna Efimchik. While initially upset, this young law firm associate takes a positive view. The second firm, she told the *American Bar Association Journal*, "did me a favor by hiring me in the first place. I've had a job for the last three and a half months, I got severance, and another great firm on the résumé."[13]

Articulate a Positive Vision of
Your Different Future

She was known simply as the Central Park Jogger: a twenty-eight-year-old New York City investment banker who was beaten, raped, and left for dead by a gang in Central Park. She was in a coma for two weeks. Her left eye socket was crushed in; she suffered a traumatic brain injury. The doctors didn't think she would survive, much less walk or talk. Fourteen years later, Trisha Meili revealed her identity in her book, *I Am the Central Park Jogger: A Story of Hope and Possibility*. She works with a track club that helps disabled athletes participate in marathons, and helps the Department of Veterans Affairs make sure injured soldiers and their families have the resources they need upon returning from war. About herself, she told *Fox News*, "Life is not over, it's not easy, it's a lot of work. There can be a lot of frustrations. Yes, it will be different. But different doesn't mean worse."[14]

Nightmares happen. In a single year, Amy Cohen lost her mother, her job, and her boyfriend, and she got a face-ravaging rash that lasted for eight months. In *Wesleyan Magazine*, she wrote that she looked as if she had fallen asleep on a George Foreman grill. Friends asked if she ever compared herself to the Bible's Job. She never learned to ride a bike when she was growing up, and at age thirty-five she bought one and started teaching herself to ride for the first time in her life. As she rode her bike, she kept telling herself, "Forward. Just go forward."[15] She has since published a best-selling memoir, *The Late Bloomer's Revolution*, and became a writer and producer for two TV sitcoms, *Caroline in the City* and *Spin City*.

Find Meaning in the Face of Death

Psychiatrist Viktor Frankl is an Auschwitz survivor. His book *Man's Search for Meaning* has sold over twelve million copies. Frankl believes the choice to find meaning in life exists for anyone, even those facing death—whether at Auschwitz or for other reasons. Based on his own experience and those of many death camp survivors, Frankl advises that the way a person accepts his or her fate and all the suffering it entails is what adds deeper meaning to life. "We who lived in concentration camps can remember the men who walked through the huts comforting others, giving away their last piece of bread. They may have been few in number but they offer sufficient proof that everything can be taken away from a man but one thing: the last of the human freedoms—to choose one's own attitude in any given circumstances, to choose one's own way."[16]

Auschwitz prisoners were talked out of suicide when they focused on what life expected from them. They included a man reminded about the child he adored who was waiting for him in a foreign country, and a scientist who had written a series of books that needed to be finished outside the death camp.[17] Frankl echoes the philosophy of German philosopher Nietzsche, who posited that *once you know the why for your existence, you will be able to bear almost any how.*[18]

At Memorial Sloan-Kettering Cancer Center in New York, a new experimental group therapy has sprung up based on the writings of Viktor Frankl. The eight-week program helps terminal cancer patients reconnect with the sources of meaning in their life: family relationships, work, and love. "We help cancer patients understand that they are not dead yet," William Breitbart, a psychiatrist who developed the program, told the *Wall Street Journal.* "The months or years of life that remain can be times of extraordinary growth."[19]

Instant Survivor™ Alert

Danny Harris and the others I've described in this chapter inspire us to know that no matter what life sends our way, our futures can still be magical. Yes, they will be different. The future will not equal the past. You may be required at some point to let go and relinquish your view of what your future was meant to be or was going to be, just as Danny Harris accepted that he would not be a millionaire and repeat Olympic champion. When trouble strikes, we might have to say good-bye to our past, but not farewell to life. We have the option to stay frosty, secure support, stand tall, and accept that the future is our friend. That is our choice.

MANAGER TIP #12—YOUR FUTURE IS YOUR FRIEND

If you have a colleague who is suffering a personal professional crisis, ask him or her this question:

Have you thought about how your future might be different but be as great as or greater than your life before this challenge came up?

• • •

Looking toward the future requires companies to consider how their core business will change and what crises these changes can precipitate. As they prepare for crises moving forward, companies need to have a firm grasp of the "soft factors" beyond profits that they are trying to preserve. How will they protect their reputation and identity? Defining and protecting these soft assets is equally important for you if you plan to be an *Instant Survivor™*.

YOUR FUTURE IS YOUR FRIEND

Choose to build a different, bright future.

- Your past does not dictate your future—unless you let it.

- Use calamity to gain clarity on what you want in life.

- Give meaning to your disaster by helping others through theirs.

- A life comeback is possible from any depth.

13

LAND OF THE LIVING DEAD

Jim Walsh, who operates Burger King and TCBY restaurants in the Dakotas and Minnesota, and who headed the Make-A-Wish Foundation in South Dakota for ten years, says, "The two most important days of your life are the day you were born and the day you figure out why you were born."[1] Companies have an especially difficult time defining their values and their mission and aligning them with their survival plans. They find it easier to take "hard" steps to prevent easily spotted dangers with actions such as providing security for their buildings; they struggle with "soft" steps for mushier challenges such as defining and preserving their reputations.

Often we can handle our "hard" prevention steps for easily identified life crises (stockpiling provisions, having some cash on hand, babyproofing our homes, etc.), but the "soft" side of preparation—to define, build, and protect our reputations (working on relationships, networking, thinking, and planning) takes more effort, and we tend to avoid it. However, it's crucial that we take the "soft" steps to protect ourselves. So let's first see what prevents us from taking these soft steps and then study what can motivate us to change our habits.

Needless Chances, Heedless Choices

The inhaling and exhaling of breaths are heard rhythmically from around the room. It's not the customary uneven, irregular breathing of a group of people. Each breath is precise: the same amount of air sucked in, held the same length of time, and released at precisely the same moment before the process starts again.

The breaths emerge from bodies positioned on their backs, immobile, except for the forced rise and fall of their chests. They are brain-dead Maryland residents. Most rode motorcycles without helmets, got into accidents, and suffered severe head injuries. They "live" on ventilators and feeding tubes at a rural Maryland state facility that treats uninsured and underinsured residents who suffered traumatic injuries.

Each mechanical breath reinforces the waste of lives and money caused when people figure they can take needless chances since disaster will not strike them. Did they picture themselves warehoused with other accident victims in a forgotten facility? Were they ready to trade a fast, "freeing" ride for their bodies or their lives?

I visited them as part of a governor's commission seeking to save taxpayers' money by making state government more efficient. One obvious step: keep in place the motorcycle helmet law that each year a small group of motorcyclists and like-minded legislators seek to overturn on "personal freedom" grounds.

"I'm no motorcycle mama."

Perhaps you read this and think, "Number one, I don't ride motorcycles, and, number two, if I ever did, I'd wear a helmet." Fair point. Even with helmets, however, severe injuries strike motorcyclists.

But before we scoff at "stupid" motorcyclists, does their approach reflect our own? They don't wear helmets to protect themselves; we don't acknowledge, prevent, and prepare for the troubles we will encounter. In fact, we sometimes figure that thinking bad thoughts will only make them more likely to occur. So we don't think about what could go wrong and how to fireproof our lives.

So, how can we protect ourselves?

First, ditch assumptions about life that rarely hold up. We believe there is permanence to our lives that defies the statistics of real life. We think our spouses, jobs, and houses or apartments will always be there. We cling to this notion despite the heavy divorce rate; the recent heavy layoffs, downsizing, and rightsizing; and the parade of home destruction from fires, hurricanes, and tornadoes we routinely see on the evening news. At a recent dinner, seven of eight men at my table were divorced.

Be realistic. As my grandfather used to say, "Trust everyone, and cut the cards." That should be your view of life. Trust that your life will work out well. But protect yourself in case it does not, which is likely.

Hard Stuff Is Easy

You probably practice crisis avoidance every day in many ways. You check the weather forecast before you get dressed. You wear a seat belt in the car. You put a flashlight and flares in your car trunk. You hide a spare key outside your residence or give one to a neighbor you trust. To get more personal, you put a condom in your wallet or a tampon in your purse. You make sure your gas tank is full in case of an emergency. You check the mirrors and signal before changing lanes. You balance your checkbook. You may have your children fingerprinted to help the police identify and recover them in case of a kidnapping. Perhaps you stock your basement with a week's worth of drinking water, dried food, and a battery-operated radio to prepare for a disaster.

We prevent common problems with a trip to the hardware or

grocery store. Did you notice that almost all those precautions involved tangible, or hard, things—keys, belts, flashlights, food? We take these easy one-time steps in an effort to prevent small, common mishaps from becoming major problems.

Soft Stuff Is Hard

But there's another set of complicated, messy, multidimensional problems that sneak up on us. Think illness, bankruptcy, divorce, job loss. No matter how many of the smart steps just listed we take, they won't halt these big-time problems or help us respond to them in a major way. No emergency provisions stored in our basements will give us an easy solution.

We prevent these major-league problems or stop them from turning into life-altering disruptions only when we work on the more challenging "soft" prevention steps: namely, fortifying relationships, building networks, and improving our lifestyles. You may notice that we can do all of the "hard" steps listed above on our own. The "soft" preparation steps require collaboration with others—bosses, coworkers, spouses, partners, friends, family. They also require us to strip away our denial, our fears, and our resistance to change and to stoke ourselves emotionally and psychologically for our challenges. We owe it to ourselves and those who rely on us to do this.

Future Fear

We resist changing our lives, even when we are unhappy or sense trouble brewing. Don't you see friends persist in dead-end jobs and relationships they admit are busts? We get comfortable with how we live and work and don't want to rock the boat. So we don't.

Why don't we work on the soft side of life? We're afraid. Whatever our reality is, at least we know it. Fear of the unknown on the other side of change keeps us from responding to trouble. Unfortunately, big hurricanes sweep away those who refuse to abandon their comfortable lives and homes. We think others will rescue us when trouble hits.

How often do we fret about the hazards of a new school, new city, new job, new boss, or new neighbor—and within weeks or months we have happily adjusted? We magnify the risk that any change poses and minimize our success in adapting to change.

There is another key crisis prevention ingredient we need—expertise. Unlike major corporations, we don't know how to stave off potentially life-altering events. We skip the "soft" actions because they are challenging and we don't know how to shore up our vulnerabilities, which means a crisis can crush us.

Think of the dangerous ingredients we mix into our lives: denial, fear, faith we'll be rescued, resistance to change, and lack of expertise. It's no surprise we skip critical crisis prevention and preparation steps. But with a prevention plan, we can banish fear of the future that imprisons us in the present.

Instant Survivor™ Alert

Think hard on whether you take an active or a passive approach to life. If it's active, crisis prevention comes more easily to you. If it's passive, you may need to work a little harder. Before we analyze how you can prevent crises in the major areas of your life, three questions help underscore why crisis prevention is critical. Ask yourself these three crucial questions: Who am I? What is my talent? Who do I live life for?

MANAGER TIP #13—LAND OF THE LIVING DEAD

If you have a colleague who is suffering a personal or professional crisis, ask him or her this question:

How are you preparing for the challenges you will probably face in the future?

"Who am I?"

While we think about ourselves constantly, we tend to focus on our wants, needs, and feelings. We don't think about who we really are and what promises we make to others and ourselves.[2] What are your three best character traits? Your most important values? Would your best friends agree? What three lines would you write about yourself on your tombstone?[3]

"What is my talent?"[4]

Do you remember the Bible story of a master who gave three talents ("talents" were ancient money) to three servants to use while he was away? Two invested and doubled the money, but the third buried the money to make sure he could return it. When the master returned, he berated the third servant for hiding from the world the "talent" he had received.

What is your talent? What passion, skill, or ability do you enjoy having and using? Does your talent sustain life for you and the people you care about?

"Who do I live life for?"

Think deeply on who you live life for. Yourself? Your parents? Your kids? Your spouse, partner, boyfriend, or girlfriend? A dead parent or relative? People you have never met or who are not yet born? For God? Is this a tough question? Finding the answer will guide you to prevent, manage, and fix your current or future life crisis.

You connect with someone else, be it a spouse, a partner, a lover, children, parents, siblings, or other significant people in your life. They depend on you to protect their futures by protecting yours. Just as pregnant women eat for two, you live for two or more people.

Think back on the brain-dead motorcyclists. Did they focus on who they were, what their talents were, and who they lived life for? Did they think how riding without a helmet could hurt them and their families? Did they consider the economic drain they would place on others, including strangers? If they thought about trouble, did they prepare for it? Buy insurance? Make a living will?

Liberating Life

Living for others may bring up the image of a pack mule bearing heavy burdens and responsibilities. But when you view yourself living your life for others, it can be liberating. It ends debate about whether you take a passive or an active approach to life and crisis prevention; it has to be active when you're trying to protect others by protecting yourself. It avoids the quarrel you have with yourself about whether you should prepare for disaster or enjoy the present and let the future take care of itself. It is not selfish to protect yourself.

When we focus on what others need us to do for them, we learn what we need to do for ourselves. They need us healthy, employed, and happy. So we need to act now to live healthy lives, fireproof our careers, solidify

LAND OF THE LIVING DEAD

- Abandon the comforting belief that life won't send trouble your way.
- Live in a positive way and protect yourself from crisis.
- Practice the easy "physical" prevention steps daily.
- Take the emotional, "soft" preparation steps after answering three questions:

  Who am I?

  What is my talent?

  Who do I live life for?

- Motivate yourself to avoid crises by realizing you live for others, not just yourself.

our close relationships, and build a network of friends and acquaintances that can help when trouble hits.

Crisis prevention does not just help save your future; it improves your present life. When you strengthen ties to friends and family, you are happier. When you raise your reputation at work, you get more recognition, job satisfaction, and higher pay. When you resolve a lingering health issue, you improve your outlook on life immediately.

Don't think of crisis prevention as an insurance policy you buy and hope you'll never need. Your crisis prevention plan—discussed in chapters fourteen and fifteen and detailed in chapter sixteen—is also a "present improvement plan." They will discuss how you can burnish your reputation and prevent and plan for trouble. By acting to save your future, you better your life today.

•   •   •

In the next chapter, we'll dig deeper into these soft issues as we explore how companies and individuals strive to protect their identity, their talent, and their purpose in life. You will learn that in many situations, what you are protecting is not much different from what major corporations are protecting. You are protecting your brand.

BUILD BRAND LOYALTY

A company answers the question "Who am I?" by highlighting its reputation and image—what marketers call its "brand." It answers the question "What is my talent?" by pointing to its distinctive products or services and its ability to generate new ones. A company answers the question, "Who do I live for?" by citing its employees, customers, and shareholders. When companies can't answer those three questions or don't uphold the values that spark their answers, they falter or fail.

Great companies can answer all three questions by citing their brands. But what is a brand, exactly? (Watch out here for corporate speak.) One brand specialist defines it as "an intangible, but critical component of what a company stands for."[1] Some view a brand as the collection of impressions made by every interaction the company has with its customers, employees, and suppliers.[2] Others say a brand is a promise to meet or exceed your expectations about the product.[3]

Think about some brands and the promises made to you. GEICO: cheaper car insurance, fast and hassle-free. Southwest: no-frills, on-time airline. Gatorade: energy drink of star athletes that makes you a champion. Consumers rely on brands to enrich, improve, and safeguard their lives.

Great brands also stand for critical values of hope, trust, and caring for those who depend on them.[4] Johnson & Johnson's founder drafted a credo of values more than sixty-five years ago that still inspires the company's approach. The remarkably farsighted credo, excerpted below, has helped J&J consistently place at the top of worldwide surveys of corporate brands:

- We believe our first responsibility is to the doctors, nurses, and patients, to mothers and fathers, and all others who use our products and services.

- We are responsible to our employees . . . everyone must be considered as an individual.

- We are responsible to the communities in which we live and work and to the world community as well.

- Our final responsibility is to our stockholders. . . . We must experiment with new ideas. Research must be carried on, innovative programs developed, and mistakes paid for.[5]

"Great taste, less filling!"

Companies spend billions promoting their brands. They hire Madison Avenue advertising and production firms, focus group consultants, and marketing maestros. Their goal: establish an emotional tie, a loyalty between you and their brands. For thirty-plus years, Miller Lite beer commercials have featured celebrities and others vociferously arguing (and in one controversial TV ad going breast-to-breast) over whether Miller Lite appeals because it "tastes great" or is "less filling." That's the archetype of consumer loyalty that companies strive to create.

When a company has a strong brand and a positive reputation, consumers will be supportive when the company makes a mistake or faces a crisis. Companies with strong reputations can survive crises.

Think about Mattel. The world's largest toy company built an enviable reputation for making safe and charming playthings, including Barbie, Sesame Street characters, and Sarge cars. Then in August 2007, the story broke that Mattel's Chinese-made toys contained lead paint. Plus, powerful magnets could break off from some toys, and if swallowed by children, bond together in their digestive tracts. The co-owner of the Chinese factory that used the lead paint hanged himself. Mattel recalled more than twenty million toys. The stock fell 13 percent. Congress dragged the CEO to Washington to testify.[6]

For many companies: lights out. But parents had a history of trusting Mattel, and the company's product recalls and CEO apologies reassured them about Mattel's safety commitment. In 2008, *Fortune* magazine named Mattel to its "100 Best Companies to Work For" list. Mattel's brand strength saved the company.

As you will see, brand strength can also serve as an invaluable asset for individuals as they face a personal or professional crisis.

A Baseball Brand

Terry Francona wanted to be a major league baseball player when he grew up. Period. His father played in the majors, and Terry, nicknamed "Tito," announced at age nine that he was going to be a big-league ballplayer too. After being a high school and college baseball standout, Tito was drafted by the Montreal Expos and played for ten seasons. Then a succession of injuries forced him to retire and he returned to his Tucson, Arizona, home.

This was crunch time for Tito. Like many professional athletes, he struggled with his next step. When I talked to him in Boston, he told me: "I didn't know what I was going to do with the rest of my life and had never really thought about it before. To be honest with you, [I] wasn't too panicked about it. Probably should have been."

Married, with three children, Tito signed up for a residential real estate course. Halfway through the course, a former Cincinnati Reds teammate, Buddy Bell, called him. Bell, then with the Chicago White Sox organization, asked Tito to become a White Sox minor league hitting instructor. Bell respected Tito from their playing days together and told him he thought he would make a good manager. Tito said he thought about Bell's offer for about ten minutes before accepting it. "I never looked back," he said.

Francona admits that if Bell hadn't called him he might never have become a team manager. "I can say that I don't know. For someone to ask you to manage, you have to be pretty fortunate [and] be in the right place at the right time. So I can't sit here and say that I'd have even approached it or that someone would have approached me. I don't know that for sure."

Think about how many major league baseball players there are who would like to manage but never get the chance? When they stop playing, their baseball days come to a crashing halt. Tito got the call because Bell believed in the "Francona brand."

America's best companies define, build, and protect their brands—that which makes them special—just as Terry Francona does and just as you can do in your life. If you think about it, companies have identities just like people do, which means we can learn from their brand prowess.

We talked about the hard questions we must answer to prevent and be prepared for a crisis: Who am I? What is my talent? Who do I live life for? Successful companies—that is, those that thrive in good times and survive crises—ask and answer the same questions.

How has Tito Francona built the sterling reputation that got him noticed before and after he retired as a player? He stays consistent during challenging times, focuses on other people, and takes bold action to win.

Stay consistent during challenging times.

Tito was a baseball vagabond, playing for five major league teams in ten years after getting injured early in his career. He described the cycle: get released (fired) by a team and then show up for the new team's spring training as a non-roster player and try to earn a spot; or, be sent to the minor leagues and try to fight your way back to the new team. During this boom-and-bust decade, Tito's wife asked him, "Aren't you getting frustrated?" Tito's response? "No, this was an opportunity. . . . I'd be so excited to even go back to Triple-A (the highest minor league division). . . . It taught me patience, and I got humbled more than one time. It really helped me being a manager."

His patience was tested early in his managerial career. Do you remember when basketball star Michael Jordan played baseball after retiring from the Chicago Bulls? You may not remember that Jordan's first stop was the Birmingham Barons, a White Sox Double-A team managed by Tito Francona. A cascade of national sports writers transformed Francona's sleepy world into a closely watched media circus. The first time Tito saw Jordan bat, Jordan popped up and skipped running out the play. Tito didn't give Jordan star treatment, asking him later that day, "Just tell me now: are you going to do that every time?" Jordan responded, "No, that will never happen again. Never."[7]

Yet Francona's life as manager of the Philadelphia Phillies was even more challenging. Francona twice had a last-place team; it always posted losing records. Even though it was widely known that the team had few strong players, the city was unforgiving. "Philadelphia is a tough place," Tito told me, "a very opinionated city." Fans dubbed him "Francoma." Was it rough showing up each day knowing the team would likely lose? "I never felt that way. I always felt we were going to win. That's just our mentality."

His last season as the Phils manager was particularly bleak. The team lost the most games in his four years as manager. Some players started to show up late for practice. Tito says he sat down the young players "to teach them how to be professionals. Sure it's more fun if you're winning, but I couldn't let go of my responsibility." Nevertheless, the city blasted Francona and the players. Tito didn't shy away from taking the heat. He says: "In a place that's very media-driven and very aggressive, I felt it was my responsibility, if the players were trying their best, to protect them at all times. . . . I felt like I shouldered a lot of responsibility, but again, that was my job, I was supposed to, so I did it the best I could." The general manager fired Tito on the last day of the season.

When Tito took over as manager of the Boston Red Sox in 2004, the city harbored two dreams: win a World Series for the first time since 1918 and beat the Yankees in the play-offs (not necessarily in that order of importance). So, count Boston players and fans as defeated, dispirited, and downcast when, in the American League Championship that year, the Red Sox lost the first three games to the despised Yankees, the last one by the humiliating tally of 19–8. After the game, Tito said he repeated his standard message to the players, telling them to come back tomorrow ready to play. He believes consistency is crucial in handling demoralizing situations. "We didn't change the lineup. We sent the same guys out there that had won ninety-eight games during the year. I remember feeling that if we're going to come back . . . we got to do it with the guys that got us here."

Focus on other people.

Tito's philosophy is simple: "I always felt when I became manager that if I put the players' and the organization's needs and wants first, my situation would always take care of itself." Let's look at three examples of how he implements that approach.

DON'T PLAY FAVORITES. When I interviewed Tito before he left as Red Sox manager, he told me, "As manager of the Red Sox, there are always people you are going to gravitate toward. But if those are the only people you have a relationship with, it doesn't make you a very good manager. The young players, the veteran players, the Spanish-speaking players, you try to build relationships with everybody because that's the only way it works."

SUPPORT YOUR STRUGGLING PLAYERS. Boston fans shouted for the scalps of two slumping players during the early losses to the Yankees in the 2004 play-off series: Johnny Damon and Mark Bellhorn. But Tito told Damon, "You're going to be leadoff [hitter] until the day I leave here." He told Bellhorn he would continue playing second base. Tito says, "If players are struggling and I run from them, I'm not doing my job." Bellhorn hit the winning home run in game six of the play-off series, Damon in game seven.

RESPECT YOUR PLAYERS BY BEING ORGANIZED. Tito admits that he's not particularly organized in his day-to-day life. Yet he's fanatical about organization as a manager. Each spring training practice segment is carefully scheduled. "I care so much about us being organized in spring training, I kid with the coaches that if we have to show up an hour early to be organized, we're going to do it. . . . I think players will work hard, they'll listen, but the minute you show that you're not organized, you've lost them."

Take bold action to win.

After losing the first three games to the Yankees in the 2004 play-off series, the Red Sox entered the ninth inning of game four down by a run and facing the Yankees' legendary relief pitcher, Mariano Rivera. Before the inning started, Tito met with the Sox's speediest base runner, Dave Roberts, in the tunnel adjacent to the field. Tito told Roberts that if the team's first hitter, Kevin Millar, got to first base, Roberts would run for him and should steal second. Millar walked and Roberts went in to run for him.

Tito's approach was fraught with risk. The standard baseball move: tell the next batter, Billy Mueller, to sacrifice himself and bunt Roberts over to second base, giving the Sox two chances to score Roberts and tie the game. I asked Tito if he thought about what would happen to him if Roberts was picked off first base or thrown out stealing, and the Sox were left with no one on base and one out. He replied: "No, not during the game. It would have been devastating. . . . I was so into the game that I had never even thought about it. But I don't doubt for one minute it would have been ugly."

Here's how Tito analyzed it. "We didn't ask Billy Mueller to bunt all year, and now all of a sudden we're getting into the most important game of the year and we're asking him to do something he hadn't done much of. So it's not a lock that it's going to work." On asking Roberts to steal, Tito had this thought in mind: "It was our best chance to win. You only get so many shots at Rivera. He is the elite closer in the league, and if you get a bunt down and you're successful, you've given them an out. And we didn't need to give him any outs; he's good enough on his own. . . . Let [Roberts] try to steal, and if he's safe, we've got a man on second with nobody out as opposed to one out, and that increases our chances."

Tito continued: "As Dave Roberts was leaving the dugout, he kind of glanced back at me, and I just winked at him. . . . And he had a big smile on his face. And I remember never in a million years thinking he would be thrown out stealing. When I look back at the video, my goodness, it was close." But Roberts successfully stole second base, Mueller singled him in to tie the game, and the Red Sox won the game in the twelfth inning. "It was just an unbelievable baseball play," Tito said.

Despite the team's historic collapse in 2011 and Tito's departure as manager, his hiring was a great play for the Boston Red Sox. When he became their manager in 2004, he led them to two World Series titles after an eighty-six-year drought.

Instant Survivor™ Alert

You are a brand, too. Think about yourself as a brand now and in the future. You don't need to become a top athlete, pop star, or Fortune 500 executive.[8] But you can be a big shot to your colleagues and friends. You'll need to make a promise to them about who you are and how you act that they can count on.

MANAGER TIP #14—BUILD BRAND LOYALTY

If you have a colleague who is suffering a personal or professional crisis, ask him or her this question:

Have you ever thought about yourself as a brand that you should work to promote and protect?

Brand yourself.

How can you shape, buff, and protect your brand so others have clear, positive feelings about you based on personal experience or reputation? To understand and develop your brand, flesh out your answer to the first of the three big questions we focused on in the last chapter, beginning with "Who am I?"

Answer the question "Who am I?" by listing your three best qualities. Before you write them down, think about who you are and how you act in the following categories: treatment of others, work ethic, personal ethics, attitude and outlook, and emotional qualities.[9]

Now examine what others—your spouse, partner, boyfriend/girl-friend, parent(s), sibling(s), children, best friend from childhood, new-est friend, spiritual leader, boss, coworkers, and the drugstore clerk or someone else who doesn't know you well—identify as your three best traits.[10] Ask them to list which three they would choose and help them answer by suggesting they consider what role you play in the commu-nity, what you are willing to fight for, and what you stand for.

What do you notice about their responses? Do they depend on how long someone has known you? Are there different answers for cowork-ers versus friends? Is there a particular attribute that everyone men-tions? Only when you understand your brand are you ready to protect, preserve, and promote it.

Create a brand promise.

Remember what a brand is: a promise to others that you meet or exceed.[11] You make a promise about who you are and what you pledge to do. After working through this process, here is how the brand descrip-tion of a person (let's call her Ms. Smith) might sound: Brand "Smith" stands for being loyal, analytical, and optimistic. Now, substitute your own last name and write down your three best qualities.[12]

A positive brand is credible, reliable, and memorable.[13] A consumer who finds the product works reliably as promised will remember the experience. Isn't your goal to generate strong, positive feelings in the people in your life? A strong personal brand will widen and deepen your circle of friends, colleagues, and acquaintances. When they trust you, they will support you when you make a mistake or face a crisis. They will come out of the woodwork to help.

Once you have a fix on your brand, ferociously protect and fortify it.

Isn't that what great leaders do? Show their coolness and bravery in tense times? That quality is not reserved for CEOs, statesmen, and sports stars. That's what our families, friends, and colleagues look to see from us. If trouble comes your way, it's your chance to bolster those who rely on you and to boost your reputation.

• • •

You have learned how to adapt the right attitude toward the future and have begun to protect your soft assets by defining your brand. Now it's time to examine how companies prevent crises by conducting an audit to determine their vulnerability in certain areas and how you can make a vulnerability audit of your own life.

BUILD BRAND LOYALTY

You are a living, breathing brand. Being a successful brand means making a promise to others that you meet or exceed.

- Discover your unique brand by identifying your three best qualities.

- Protect, improve, and buff your brand.

- Live your brand and it will protect you in times of crisis.

HEAR THE ALARM BELLS

You remember the oil filter ad that warned, "You can pay me now or pay me later." Companies have decided it is cheaper to pay up front to protect themselves from crises. A Houston Advanced Research Center study concluded that each dollar spent on disaster preparedness saves seven dollars in losses.[1]

So how do companies prevent crises? They undertake a threat assessment plan (also referred to as a vulnerability audit). They review their policies, procedures, and operations to identify current and potential weaknesses that could trigger a crisis. Their goal: to detect the early warning signs of trouble on the horizon so they can stop it or at least be better prepared to respond to it.

A vulnerability audit has three phases: threat identification, threat review, and threat response. An outside consultant or law firm typically helps to lend objectivity and provide a speedy turnaround.

Before describing in detail how a corporate vulnerability audit works, let's see why it matters.

Several years ago a Fortune 500 manufacturing company (which I won't name) had never before faced a significant crisis, but it decided to conduct a full-scale vulnerability audit. In the following two years, unexpected crises rained down on it: a tornado, a major lawsuit, a union organizing campaign, a product recall, and a possible embezzlement.

The corporation says the audit enabled it to respond quickly and effectively to all of these challenges.

Phase One: The Scrub Down

Think of phase one as a scrub down. How do companies do the scrubbing? The crisis team reviews the company's key crisis preparedness and response documents such as the disaster and emergency response plans. They talk to insurance brokers and industry associations to determine the latest trends in lawsuits filed against companies by whistle-blowers and other plaintiffs.

Then they interview the company's key people who can best prevent or respond to a crisis and run the company during one. They ask about past crises faced by the company and its competitors. By sorting through what caused those crises, they learn what could have prevented them and what fixes were made to ensure that they wouldn't happen again. They check out what corporate practices draw flak from company regulators. They study what hot company or industry issues attract media scrutiny.

Asking employees to play "what-if" helps identify the worst-case scenarios the company is likely to face. They drill down with employees, looking for skeletons in the closet and other hidden risks that could trigger a crisis. The list will include such events as a facility explosion, a data breach, an embezzlement, terrorism, the death of a key executive, illegal payments, financial irregularities, natural disasters, a labor strike, and a consumer boycott.

Phase Two: Hit Parade of Horrors

Companies often pick the top ten threats to examine in detail. They study them closely: why and how they can occur, what damages they would cause, and how the company's employees, customers, and the media are likely to react to them.

They rank the events by analyzing the probable impact of each one on the company. They ask employees to judge how severe each event might be. They calculate how each event would affect operations, the attention it would receive from regulators and the media, and the damage it would cause to the bottom line and the company's reputation.

Next, they assign a number between 1 and 10 to the probable impact of each event (with 10 being the most severe). Then they assign a number between 1 and 10 for the probability of each event occurring (with 10 being certain to occur). After multiplying those two numbers together for each event, they rank the crises, starting with the highest number.

Phase Three: Break Glass

The final phase judges the company's ability to respond to each of the top ten threats. After developing ideal responses to these threats and then assessing whether the company can respond under stress, the company strengthens vulnerable areas.

•   •   •

BP offers a positive example of how the corporate vulnerability audit process works. Schooled on the Exxon Valdez disaster, BP knew it also risked an oil spill and realized that it had better be prepared when the disaster struck. In 1989, the international oil and gas giant wrote a crisis management plan designed to get themselves ready to respond should anything go awry.

"This time, they were ready."

When thousands of gallons of BP oil spilled off the coast of California one year later and washed up on the Orange County coastline, the company broadcast its readiness to confront the spill. It quickly provided video footage of three thousand BP employees cleaning oil off the rocks. Even though another company actually owned the tanker that spilled the oil, the BP CEO did not duck responsibility, acknowledging on the *Today* show, "It is our oil." ABC TV's anchor Peter Jennings announced on the evening news, "This time, they were ready."[2] The mixed crisis record of oil companies highlights why vigilance must be constant, not occasional.

Leading companies constantly scan for trouble. By spotting looming issues, they neutralize them or position a response. Defense contractors get ready for Capitol Hill hearings on wartime contracting. Clothing chains are on high alert to stop suppliers from using child labor or polluted cotton. Bad parts from China make toy manufacturers vigilant.

Companies address the impact on their businesses of a variety of societal issues, such as climate change, globalization, and terrorism, to name a few. They identify and resolve what can spell trouble: lax accounting controls, minimal control over suppliers and contractors, easy employee access to confidential information. An effective early warning and response system avoids major losses and headaches when a natural or man-made crisis strikes.

Isn't that what we want to do in our personal and professional lives? Win the battle before it's fought?

Instant Survivor™ Alert

How can you protect and defend your brand against major threats before they morph into full-blown crises? The same way companies do. As we discussed, companies perform a three-step vulnerability audit.

They first spot looming threats. They review the most dangerous ones in detail. Then they correct the weaknesses they uncover to prevent those threats from turning into crises.

You can do the same thing. By undertaking a vulnerability audit of both your personal and your professional life, you can examine the particular threats you face. Then you can correct problems you identify during your audit before they transform from minor headaches to migraines—or worse.

MANAGER TIP #15—HEAR THE ALARM BELLS

If you have a colleague who is suffering a personal or professional crisis, ask him or her this question:

Are you working to spot problems before they become crises so you can correct weaknesses and shore up vulnerabilities?

You will need a "kit" to do your audit. First, buy a reporter or stenographer's notebook: one of those small, flip ones you can carry in your purse, briefcase, or shoulder bag. You'll fill your notebook with evaluations and action plans that are described in the next chapter. (Don't use a three-ring notebook. Why not? Just think of the many notebooks created with great intentions that rest undisturbed on your shelves at home or at work.) You'll also need a kitchen timer or stopwatch.

Before you conduct your life audit, let's do some warm-up exercises.

Write down a one-sentence description of your brand in your notebook (if you don't have the right notebook yet, just use a piece of paper). Do it by completing the sentence on the following page.

HEAR THE ALARM BELLS

Copy the approach companies take to protecting their brands:

- Boost your brand to build loyalty.
- Don't wait until disaster hits.
- Conduct a thorough vulnerability audit.
- Identify and rank the major brand threats.
- Examine the major threats in detail.
- Strengthen your ability to respond to these threats.

Brand _____ (fill in your last name) stands for _____. If you aren't ready to fill in the blank, turn back to chapter fourteen and answer the questions that help you describe your brand. Please don't skip this step. Defining your brand helps you understand who you are, what you have to protect, and why it matters.

Brand Ambushes

Now identify a few personal and professional crises that could ambush your brand. What could go wrong in your life? What are the biggest threats that could be life altering? Think big. Forget small stuff. If your car muffler's kaput, get it fixed. Think about threats that could disrupt your life.

You need to use your "radar" to save you from brand threats. Early detection helps you avoid or minimize them.

Your radar won't work all the time, however. Some threats are silent killers (and produce no warning signs before striking). Others are hard to spot at the time. Some disasters fall in the "life is random" category; just ask the passengers who were on board the plane Captain "Sully" Sullenberg crash-landed in the Hudson River.

Skip denial and disbelief as you do this. Think of the victims surprised by Bernie Madoff, Hurricane Katrina, and the Enron bankruptcy. Forget thinking "that'll never happen" or "that won't be a big deal." Write down what you know could happen to you because you have seen it happen in your family, neighborhood, workplace, or community. List what you consider to be your top five threats. In the next chapter, we'll examine key steps you can take to reduce your vulnerabilities in the critical areas of your life.

* * *

Congratulations. You have learned how companies protect their brands from crises and how you can copy their approach. Companies have a well-defined system for conducting a vulnerability audit. You have begun to use that system by defining your brand and listing potential threats to your brand. Now we're ready to start on an even bigger challenge—completing your life audit.

COMPLETE YOUR LIFE AUDIT

Now that your "audit motor" is running, let's go ahead and conduct a three-phase audit in the four big areas of your life: job/career, finances, health, and relationships.

You can protect your future and improve your present life with this audit. By storing the audit results in your notebook and identifying critical actions to take in each area, you will have begun a life improvement and protection plan that will be within easy reach. Here's how to do it.

Phase One

For each key life area, evaluate the area's current status and give it a rating between 1 and 10, with 1 meaning you believe it's in terrible shape and 10 meaning you feel it's in great shape. I'll give you some thoughts about how to evaluate each area as we go along. You will write down in your notebook the rating you give to each of the four life areas.

Phase Two

For each key life area, identify and list current and potential threats and their likelihood. Then group together the threats to each area and give each group an overall rating anywhere between 1 and 10: a 1 rating if the collection of threats is severe, and a 10 rating if you judge them to be trivial.

Then for each area, multiply the current status rating from Phase One times the overall threat rating from Phase Two. List those numbers next to each life area. The areas with the lowest numbers pose the greatest risk to your brand and therefore need the most attention.

Phase Three

Identify and list steps that will enable you to counteract the key threats in each area so you won't get ambushed.

Here's a summary of what you are going to do:

YOUR AUDIT FOR EACH LIFE AREA		
Phase One	Phase Two	Phase Three
Assess current status	Identify overall threats	Identify steps to stop threats
Assign 1–10 rating	Assign 1–10 rating	Multiply your Phase One and Phase Two ratings (your lowest life area number poses the greatest threat to you)

Now you need your timer. For each of the four life areas, I want you to spend fifteen minutes doing your three-phase audit (so you'll spend an hour total on your life audit).

Your Job/Career

Let's get started by reviewing your work life.

Phase One

Tell me how your career and job are going. Where do you stand right now? Would the judges by the side of the pool hold up 1 cards (meaning belly flop) or 10 cards (meaning gold medal winner) or something in between?

Let me throw some questions at you that might help you decide.

JOB HISTORY. How long have you held this job? Is it in the same line of work as your previous job? If not, did you make the choice to move or did you get forced out of your previous job? Is this a job or career that you trained for or took extra education for? Are you happy with your job and career choice?

JOB SUCCESS. What's your work trajectory—up, down, or sideways? Have you recently gotten a new title, more responsibility, or higher pay? Have any of your peers? How do you get along with your colleagues and your boss or bosses? Do you get formal reviews and/or informal feedback? What are you hearing?

JOB EXPERTISE. How well do you know your job and your company and industry? Are you visible outside your cubicle, office, or workstation? Do colleagues ask for your advice or guidance about your area of expertise? Do you speak about your expertise either inside or outside the company?

Write down your career and job status rating from 1–10 (1 being the worst, 10 being the best) in your notebook.

Phase Two

What are the major threats to your job and career? They are the dreaded three "Ds": being demoted, derailed, or dismissed. List them in your notebook right now, and any others you think of.

Your radar should be up for warning signs coming from two areas related to your job: your on-the-job performance and your company's overall status. You have to pay attention to both. Many successful, valued employees have gotten bounced from their jobs in the last several years not because of any mistakes they made or issues they had but because their companies failed or faltered during the downturn.

WHAT'S YOUR ATTITUDE AT WORK? Are you on autopilot at work?[1] Do you just show up, do the work, and head home? Are you there in body but not in mind and spirit? Are you, in effect, wearing headphones and blinders while you're there? If so, you're putting your job at risk because you won't be seen as a valuable contributor, you won't get a promotion, and you will make yourself a prime downsizing candidate. Also, your radar signal will be down. This means you'll miss the vibes about which employees are up or down, including you, which means you may be missing the flashing signals that your job is at risk.

HOW ARE YOU TREATED AT WORK? Are you a go-to person or are you left out of meetings and trips? Do you remember how bad you felt as a kid when the captain picked you last to play on a pickup team? It's worse when you're not picked at all. Has the company reduced your job responsibilities, budget, or direct reports? Anything related to your job with a negative sign in front of it spells trouble. Do you receive poor or neutral performance evaluations or get rapped for a poor attitude? Are you getting fewer positive training opportunities? Have you taken a remedial course, such as anger management, at the company's request? The list of trouble signs on the job is virtually limitless.[2] But if one or more of these is occurring, watch out. Make some job protection moves and get ready for a new job, both of which we will discuss how to do in this chapter.

HOW SOLVENT IS YOUR COMPANY? Job cuts and expense cutbacks are obvious red flags. Look out for a flurry of closed-door meetings and the departure of key colleagues for better jobs. Keep an eye on the finance people; they see trouble first, and if the spring is out of their step it's a sure sign of trouble. Keep abreast of the industry. Are your competitors winning more contracts and gaining market share at your expense? If the ship is going down, get in the first lifeboat and get away to a new company as quickly as possible. If a major-league scandal is brewing, leave. You don't get extra credit from potential new employers for going down with the old ship, and you get punished for staying too long with a crooked operation.

Tote up the current or future threats to your job and career and assign a 1–10 rating (1 means volcano smoke or earthquake tremors, 10 means no worries). Put that number in your notebook and then multiply it by the Phase One number to get an overall job and career threat rating.

Phase Three

What can you do about these threats? How can you improve your chances of keeping your job or finding a new one if necessary? The short answer to both questions is the same: buff your brand by increasing your involvement and visibility both on the job and outside of work.

ARE YOU HONING YOUR BRAND? Volunteer to take on more responsibility at work. Attend and participate in more meetings (even those outside your area).[3] Lend a hand to colleagues who need help on their projects while letting them claim credit. Help in any way you can to win new clients and customers: a revenue contributor is a favored employee. Listen to your colleagues' gripes and offer empathy and guidance. Get additional education or a certification. These steps are guaranteed brand boosters.

You also need to burnish your brand outside of work. When job trouble surfaces, you want a network of friends to call on who know who you are, what you do at work and in the community, and what you want to do in your career. How do you build that network? It occurs when you know others well and what they are looking for in their personal and professional lives. You will help them accomplish their goals by introducing them to a useful person or resource or sending them an article relevant to their job, company, or industry. You will get to know them socially and by working side-by-side with them doing volunteer work. You will show yourself to be capable, honest, and reliable.

ARE YOU BAGGING THE VOTES? Do you know who matters to your success at work? Are you building ties to them—by helping them directly, interacting with them socially, or connecting with them through your brand? You need their votes to move up from your current job or to keep it during tough times. Before I was voted on for partner at my firm, I headed the summer associates committee, which gave me the opportunity to take every summer associate to lunch. Guess who I invited to go with me? Every partner I felt that I didn't know well or that I wanted to get to know better. You should be networking within your industry before you need a job; other people like talking about themselves and what they do.

ARE YOU BENDING LIKE GUMBY? By "bending," I'm not talking about yielding to others' demands; I'm talking about being flexible, that is, taking on assignments, tasks, and projects outside your group and even moving to another city or overseas for work if necessary.

List in your notebook these and methods ways you think of to counteract the threats you face on the job and in your career.

Suppose despite your efforts you see the axe coming your way. If you're going to get bounced out of your job, here are a few pointers: (1) Put out job feelers to recruiters and your contacts right away; (2) line up references outside the company; (3) refresh your résumé; (4) increase your emergency fund to tide you over during unemployment; (5) do your final assignments well.

When the axe falls, build bridges; don't burn them. Personally say good-bye to all your close colleagues and supervisors, and ask a couple of them if they will provide a reference for you. Don't ignore your feelings of betrayal, embarrassment, and failure. Talk them out, shout them out, with close friends. But don't let them prevent you from moving quickly to tap your network for help.

Too many job seekers get caught in the allure of the Web. Yes, it can provide jobs, but statistics say *75 percent of jobs come from personal networking.* And don't pretend that you haven't lost your job. Finally, make smart financial steps. Continue your health care coverage with COBRA. Apply for unemployment. Identify short-term or part-time jobs you can take as you job hunt.

The timer just rang, so your fifteen minutes are up. Let's move on to your financial picture.

Your Finances

What is the taboo topic of our times? Forget sex, religion, and politics. The boundaries on those burst long ago. What is the off-limits, big secret in our lives? Our salaries and our net worth. Why? I think it's because our parents didn't talk to us about money and we duplicate that approach.

We know we have to talk with our children about sex—that's life and death these days. But we're embarrassed to discuss our financial situation with our sons and daughters because we're worried our friends and neighbors or their friends' parents have higher salaries and more money. We also worry that we will broadcast our lack of financial literacy in front of friends and neighbors who know more than we do (or at least pretend to). We decide the safe course is to shut up and lie low. Often, we don't even talk about our financial situation with our spouse or partner. By doing an "audit" of your financial picture, I hope it will help generate useful discussions with those you care about.

Phase One

After the last several years of busts, bankruptcies, and blowouts, it probably seems like a wise-guy question to ask, "So how are you doing financially?" We all got hit. But in answering the question, don't get hung up on portfolio envy. To be sure, there are a lot of investors whose portfolios are bigger than yours and mine. We need to put aside that measuring stick.

Because the key question is, "How are you doing in supporting your life?" When answering that question, it doesn't matter whether your salary is five figures, six figures, or higher. It doesn't matter whether you rent or own. Instead, three things determine whether you can support your life and the people who depend on you: a roof over your head, a steady income, and a safety net to catch you when trouble hits or you retire.

So let's stop there before we obsess about our neighbor's new fancy car or our brother-in-law's new boat. How do you stack up on the financial basics I just mentioned: housing, steady income, and a strong safety net? Give yourself a 1–10 rating (with 1 being disaster and 10 being "all set.")

Phases Two and Three

Let's talk about Phases Two and Three together because the threats and their countermeasures are so closely linked.

When it comes to our finances, we get in *over* our heads because we have no fixed guiding financial principles *in* our heads. We jeopardize our current and future standard of living by doing things that are unnecessary, unwarranted, and unwise.

I believe we get in trouble financially because we don't know or ignore the top five financial killers. They are (drum roll please):

- Too much spending

- Too much debt

- Too little investment diversification/too many exotic investments

- Too little cash on hand

- Too little insurance

Let's review each of these finance-busters closely to hammer home why you must avoid them.

Too much spending. President Calvin Coolidge said, "There is no dignity quite so impressive, and no independence quite so important, as living within your means."[4] Before he died, Ed McMahon, comedian Johnny Carson's sidekick, admitted he handled money poorly. He told CNN's Larry King, "Well, if you spend more money than you make, you know what happens. And it can happen."[5]

Too much debt. Those three words explain why so many Americans got crushed in the recent financial crash. Too much mortgage, home equity, and credit card debt meant they couldn't keep up when their mortgage rates kicked up, housing prices fell, and the struggling economy meant lower or no salaries.

Here's how you can avoid that downward spiral: don't overborrow. Rent until you can afford to buy a house. Buy a small house to start. Pay credit card bills each month on time. Don't borrow from your 401(k) or any other retirement plan or any equity you build up in your house. I know this sounds hard or unrealistic, but we know it makes sense. It's really a simple equation: overborrowing results from overspending. *If you overborrow, dig out fast.* Refinance or sell your house and move to a cheaper one. Pay off your credit card debt—highest interest rate ones first. Cut back your expenses across as many categories as possible. If that doesn't do the job, then cut out certain categories of expenses entirely.

Too little investment diversification/too many exotic investments. Your goal is to save at least 10 percent of your income (more if you can swing it) and invest it. But be smart: don't invest it all in one place. Ask formerly rich investors in Bernie Madoff's fund (who made the mistake of riding, not driving, the bus) whether putting all their eggs in one investment basket was a good idea. Ask the Wall Street whiz kids, who should definitely have known better, what results they got with too little investment diversification. The *Wall Street Journal* reports that at the end of 2006, Merrill Lynch employees had 27 percent of their retirement money in Merrill shares and lost $670 million on those holdings in 2007; twelve out of every one hundred people whose 401(k)s can hold company stock have at least 60 percent of their retirement money invested in it.[6]

The solution? **Have a mix of stocks and bonds or stock and bond funds and money market investments.** Read the previous sentence again. Make it your investment plan. The right mix of these investments is determined by your age, need for liquidity, and risk profile. I won't promise excellent short-term investment results with this technique; the market dropped about 50 percent in virtually all asset classes from September 2007 to March 2009. But diversification avoids the devastation caused by having all investments lost in a Madoff fraud or mismanaged fund. A 50 percent loss sounds great compared to a 100 percent wipeout.

Likewise, **avoid exotic investments.** Peter Lynch, the fabled Vanguard investment manager, advised everyday investors to "invest in what you know." That can be more complicated than it sounds. I prefer a simpler directive: "Don't invest in what you don't know." If you can't explain what the investment is and how it works and why it's right for you, then drop it like a hot rock. This means if you are in naked options, inverse floaters, or pork belly futures, get educated about them at one hundred miles an hour or sell them right now and invest in the safer stuff discussed above. Also, if you can't price all of your investments easily on a daily basis, watch out. This means if you're not an investment professional and you're invested in illiquid investments like hedge funds, private equity, venture capital, or real estate investment partnerships, look for the exit door.

Too little cash on hand. You need to have enough cash on hand to handle such emergencies as job loss, medical expenses, and help for sick relatives. A standard rule of thumb is to set aside six months' income in cash or liquid investments.

Too little insurance. You need to protect against the loss of or a big drop in your income. Buy enough term life insurance so your family or partner can survive your premature death and enough disability insurance to survive a catastrophic injury. If you're a small business owner or you hold significant real estate assets, then insurance can help cover estate taxes when you die.

If you avoid these five big financial killers, you will stand tall when others are falling down or sliding financially. The warning signs of a financial meltdown are easier to spot than other dangers in your life. If you're behind on paying your credit card bills, Capital One won't be shy about letting you know. If you fall behind on your mortgage, your lender will be your new pen pal. The other pressures are less obvious, but they are just as important to pick up. Watch for common warning signs (e.g, you are constantly worried about whether you can pay the bills or you and your spouse or partner regularly fight about money). Look at these five big threats as a group and give yourself a 1–10 rating (use the same scale as in Phase One). Multiply that rating by your Phase One rating to gauge your overall financial threats.

Bing! Time is up. List these threats and countermeasures in your notebook and move on to your health.

Your Health

It's time to scrutinize your health and how your lifestyle contributes to its quality.

Phase One

The old adage is that health troubles are indiscriminate. They hit old and young, rich and poor alike. But in fact, disease, death, and disability do discriminate: minority groups experience higher rates in all three of those areas than do whites. Rural residents die in more accidents and commit suicide more than urban dwellers do. A *Parade* magazine article titled "Who Gets Sick in America—And Why" reveals the health statistics that indicate various racial, ethnic, and demographic minorities face different health challenges.[7]

So, when you judge your health and your risks, start by looking at your background and your family history of disease, death, and disability (and especially if several family members have suffered a particular disease). Then review your own health: your past history and what you've learned from recent medical checkups.

I spoke to Michael Newman, MD, a highly regarded specialist in internal medicine in Washington, DC (who, I'm pleased to say, is my doctor!), about what he believes the key factors are in a person's lifestyle that affect their health. He mentioned eight factors and made the following brief points about each:

- Diet—get adequate fiber and good quality protein and avoid glycemic carbohydrates (e.g., sugared cereal).

- Weight—keep your body mass index below the overweight/obese ranges, or risk diabetes.

- Exercise—regular physical activity makes a positive difference at any age.

- Tobacco use—forget about it, or risk multiple cancers.

- Alcohol—drinking a glass or two of wine is fine, but otherwise, keep consumption minimal.

- Sleep—focus on whether you wake feeling refreshed, not on the number of hours you sleep.

- Engagement/Involvement—being engaged in life and involved in projects is good for your mental health.

- Outlook—adopt the viewpoint that life will work out.

Rate your health from 1–10 (1 means deathbed, 10 means Olympic athlete).

Phase Two

Let's forget thinking about how many diseases you could suffer. It's pointless. What is critical is to spot the warning signs, the alarm bells that your health is failing—and to do something about it. Dr. Newman advises his patients, "Your health is my concern, but your responsibility."

Many people, particularly men, "sit on" troublesome health signals rather than getting them checked. The biggest danger to your health that you can control is *you*. We generate health problems by poor diet, by lack of exercise, and by ignoring the flashing lights. Here are some classic signs:

- You regularly take days off from work because of illness but avoid seeing a doctor.

- You soldier on and ignore nagging health problems.

- You don't schedule or skip regular medical/dental checkups.

- You ignore your doctor's advice, such as refusing to take prescribed drugs.

Rate the collective threats to your health, give it a 1–10 rating (use the same scale as in Phase One), and multiply it against the Phase One rating to get your overall health threat status.

Phase Three

The basic steps to protect your health are simple: (1) Get regular checkups; (2) get treatment when serious symptoms first arise; (3) follow your doctor's advice and pay attention to your diet, exercise, and other lifestyle factors; (4) take drugs prescribed for you.

I'm not a doctor and don't play one on TV. But like you, I've dealt with lots of doctors, for me and for my family. Most of the medical care has been excellent. But disasters have occurred when I've been a doctor's doormat: I didn't know exactly what was going to be done to me, I didn't pin down exactly what symptoms I'd have and how I'd feel after the treatment, and I didn't know how much it was going to cost. So, ask questions until you're satisfied with the answers. Friends don't let friends go to the hospital alone. Bring a buddy who writes down what the doctors and nurses tell you and who can be your advocate.

Think, too, about your spiritual health. Are you protecting that—by enjoying nature or doing yoga or heading to church, temple, or another place of worship?

Before you move on to examining your relationships, list in your notebook the key steps to protect your health.

Your Relationships

Our lives revolve around our crucial relationships: boss-employee, parent-child, sibling-sibling, husband-wife, partner-partner, lover-lover. I left this topic for last because relationships are unique and there are few hard-and-fast principles for protecting and sustaining them.

To help our discussion, I checked in with two of the leading psychiatrists in Washington, DC, Dr. Catherine May and Dr. Lucy Pugh. Both women see many couples whose marriages are in trouble. Because so many people are married and bump up against problems, I decided to focus our discussion there, but much of the advice applies to all forms of relationships.

Phase One

How should couples judge the state of their marriage? Both doctors emphasized the same three guideposts:

1. Do they communicate well with each other?

One rule remains true, no matter how many times you have heard it: deep communication is the lifeblood of successful relationships. The doctors emphasized that keeping a balance in marital communication is critical. That balance means couples should not be either mute or endless chatterboxes about their lives and issues. Instead, both should speak roughly an equal and appropriate amount; important conversations need to be well timed during the day and well phrased. Communications should regularly cover problems but, at the same time, reinforce the good features of the marriage.

2. Do they solve problems well together?

Dr. Pugh poses these questions: "If a couple disagrees, how do they address it? Do they fight? Is one person passive-aggressive? Is one person always bringing up a problem while the other one avoids it? And once a conflict is identified, how do they try to solve it?"

Dr. May says that couples who solve problems well speak up sooner rather than later about issues, don't complain without a solution, and propose solutions that address the needs of both spouses.

3. Do they acknowledge and express their feelings?

Both doctors stressed that couples often struggle to explain to each other how they are feeling. Fear, pain, or embarrassment often keeps couples from having direct, honest discussions about what is bothering them or making them unhappy. "Confrontation is difficult," says Dr. May, "because very often in people's experience, confrontation ends in catastrophe," such as the breakup of a relationship or marriage.

If you're married, then give your marriage a 1–10 rating (1 signifying junkyard dogs and 10 meaning a supremely well-adjusted couple). If you're not married, then pick an important relationship in your life and use these criteria to grade it.

Phase Two

The threats to a marriage come from both internally created and externally existing forces, or "stressors" in psychiatric parlance. Simply put, couples create their own problems inside their marriage and must react to threats from outside their marriage, such as aging parents, a national recession, and natural disasters. Psychiatrists May and Pugh examine how couples respond to these stressors and look for such classic trouble signs as:

- One spouse is hiding something from the other.

- One spouse blames everything bad that happens on the other.

- A spouse repeats a destructive pattern developed from poor interactions with parents or siblings or past lovers.

- The spouses are leading separate, parallel lives.

- One spouse wants to try couples therapy and the other refuses.

Look hard at the internal and external threats to your marriage or other critical relationship and your responses to those threats. Rate your relationship on a 1–10 scale (1 equals tsunami; 10 equals Disney movie). Multiply your Phase One and Two ratings to see your overall threat picture.

Phase Three

Successful couples fend off threats to their marriage by watching how they interact with each other and other family members; being disciplined and honest in their communications; and remaining open to using others to help them work through trouble. Both doctors noted that spouses need to avoid adopting fixed, destructive roles such as "the child disciplinarian," the "nag," or "the martyr." Life partners need to talk each day about minor issues, resolve problems with "hot" topics like sex and money, and take time away together from their jobs and children. They should enjoy separate and joint constructive relationships outside the marriage.

In the face of trouble, one spouse should step up and analyze the issue, discuss it, and help identify a solution. Finally, couples can use a third party—be that good soul a neighbor, a friend, or a therapist—to remove the "electric charge" when it builds up in their relationship.

Now, write down in your notebook the steps you can take to bolster your marriage or other important relationship.

MANAGER TIP #16—COMPLETE YOUR LIFE AUDIT

If you have a colleague who is suffering a personal or professional crisis, ask him or her this question:

Have you considered doing a one-hour personal life audit?

•   •   •

Whew! You're done with your life audit. Now step back and look at how you stack up on the four key areas of your life. What areas have high ratings? Low ratings? Review the steps you can take right now to improve the low ratings and maintain the high ones.

•   •   •

Life audits such as the one you just completed have saved corporations billions of dollars. If you follow the three-phase auditing process I propose, you will avoid many crises in your personal and professional lives, short-circuit minor problems before they become major threats, and be empowered to take on and fix your vulnerabilities. But in order to be able to do this, you will have to prepare yourself to take appropriate action when faced with a crisis. In other words, you will have to train.

COMPLETE YOUR LIFE AUDIT

Identify the personal and professional threats that could ambush your brand.

Detect early signals of trouble and correct the problems.

Consider four key areas of your life:

Job/Career

Finances

Health

Relationships

Conduct a life audit of each area:

Phase 1: Rate the overall condition

Phase 2: Rate the overall risk

Phase 3: Repair your vulnerabilities

THE TRAINED SURVIVE

On a sunny morning several years ago, a sixty-two-year-old Vietnam vet nicknamed "Hard Corps" manned his desk in a New York City skyscraper. A movie buff, he'd gotten up at 4:30 that morning after spending the previous night watching movies with his wife, Susan. She had selected a blue shirt, pinstriped suit, and red silk tie for him to wear that day. They'd kissed good-bye. He called her at 8:15 a.m. from his office and told her that he loved her and that he didn't need to watch movies because he had her.[1]

The life that brought Hard Corps to his desk on that day had been tumultuous. He grew up in a British tin-mining town. He never met his father. As a teenager, he became a British paratrooper and served in conflict-torn Cyprus and Rhodesia before joining Scotland Yard as an elite detective. The pull of the Vietnam War brought him to America as a mercenary. He completed basic training at Fort Dix, New Jersey, and shipped off to Vietnam. As a second lieutenant, he led a platoon in Bravo Company of the 2nd Battalion of the 7th Cavalry—the same outfit as General Custer's at Little Bighorn. His men called him Hard Corps because he seemed nonchalant about death.[2] The book *We Were Soldiers Once . . . and Young* lauded him as a "battlefield legend," while the book *Heart of a Soldier* lionized his service to his countries.

The Seven Ps

A few years before that deceptively sunny, clear-skied day, Hard Corps, then director of corporate security for his company, had warned his higher-ups that the building wasn't safe. Hard Corps had hired Dan Hill, a fellow Vietnam solider and Special Operations veteran, to assess the building's security. Hill advised Hard Corps that the building's height exposed it to a terrorist attack. Hard Corps recommended to his bosses that the company should move to a safer location outside the city. Unfortunately, they didn't follow his prescient advice.

Hill told me that Hard Corps turned his attention to trying to protect as many employees as possible in the event of a disaster. He put in place a detailed disaster plan. He installed "evacuation" fans in the stairwells that would blow smoke out of them so that in the event of fire or attack employees would not suffocate to death. He added lights in the stairwells, powered by a backup generator, and had light strips affixed to the fronts of all the stairs. He assigned employees to be office and floor wardens and preassigned paired buddy teams that would evacuate together.

Periodically, Hard Corps led employees through evacuation drills from the large building they occupied. They then assembled away from the building where Hard Corps and his staff insisted on getting an accurate count. When employees complained, the former Vietnam platoon leader cited his seven Ps: Proper Prior Planning and Preparation Prevents Poor Performance.

Shortly after 8:47 that morning, Hard Corps received a call from the seventy-first floor in his building alerting him of a spreading fireball in the adjacent building—One World Trade Center. Immediately a loudspeaker announcement in the second tower advised everyone not to leave the building. An official from the Port Authority (the World Trade Center owner) called Hard Corps to tell him there was no danger and everyone should stay put. Hard Corps called his Vietnam vet buddy

Dan Hill and relayed what he had replied to the Port Authority official: "Piss off, you son of a bitch . . . I'm getting my people the f *** out of here."

Out Alive

Without hesitation, Hard Corps ordered all 2,700 Morgan Stanley employees, lodged on floors forty-four to seventy-one in the second tower, to evacuate. The employees walked down the stairways, two abreast, just as they had practiced—with Hard Corps calmly giving directions by bullhorn. By the time the second plane hit the second tower, many Morgan Stanley employees had exited the stricken building that would soon collapse. All but six made it out alive.[3]

Hard Corps called Hill a second time. Now Hill warned him to get out of the building. Hard Corps argued that he still had time since the first tower hadn't yet fallen. Hill explained to me that he told Hard Corps the second plane hit his tower harder, putting it at risk of coming down imminently.

FINAL ANALYSIS: Hard Corps's well-prepared plans and coolheaded, rapid response saved thousands of lives. During the evacuation, he had the presence of mind to call Susan and tell her, "You've got to stop crying. . . . If something happens to me, I want you to know that you made my life." Shortly afterward, Dan Hill and Susan stayed in contact by phone, each watching the unfolding horror on TV, when they saw the second tower collapse.

Hard Corps had headed to the upper floors to try to find stragglers. No sign of his body was ever recovered.

POSTMORTEM: Susan told me that it rained heavily the day before 9/11 and her husband had come home in a soaked suit. That suit never went to the dry cleaners. As little comfort as that is to her today, Susan can still catch a whiff of the scent of the hero who was her husband. Rick Rescorla—Hard Corps—is one of the unsung heroes of 9/11.

The Ship Passed On

Let's look at the saga of another military veteran. Tim Sears woke up around midnight in the Gulf of Mexico. Literally. He had fallen off a cruise ship, blacked out, and found himself in the water wearing boxers, a T-shirt, and a sweatshirt. It was dark save for the stars. He didn't know how he had ended up there, and the cruise ship didn't notice he was gone.

Using every swimming stroke he knew—back, side, breast, and dog paddle—he stayed afloat until dawn. He then spotted ships in the distance, but they didn't see him. Despite sunburn, fatigue, and dehydration, he was alive in the late afternoon when he saw a cargo ship heading in his direction. He tore his yellow T-shirt into pieces and waved them and shouted at the ship. The ship passed on. But then a smaller boat from the ship headed back and saved him.

In *The Survivors Club*, Ben Sherwood recounts Tim's tale. How did Tim survive seventeen hours in the water? A major factor was the discipline and mental toughness he gained from military training: he served four years as a specialist with the 82nd Airborne Division.[4]

. . .

Morgan Stanley's minimal loss of life and Tim's survival underscore that training and preparation can produce great results. We intuitively appreciate the crucial role that training plays in crisis situations. How did US Airways pilot "Sully" Sullenberger land a plane safely in the Hudson River? Training. How did NASA return the *Apollo 13* crewmen safely back to Earth? Training. How did the Secret Service agents quickly whisk President Ronald Reagan to nearby George Washington Hospital for surgery after he was shot? Training. Training is what enables people confronting a crisis to remain calm, banish fear, focus on the task at hand, and save themselves (and those around them).

Think of how many professionals rely on training. There's spring training—for six weeks, major league baseball players get ready for the season; basic training—for six months, Army recruits endure grueling exercises and drills to be combat-ready; and firearms training—FBI agents and other law enforcement officers are tested regularly on the gun range to name a few examples.

"Train to the edge and . . . lean over."

The Secret Service is built on training. To become an agent, a hopeful applicant must endure sixteen weeks of brutal training. "We train unlike any other federal agency," assistant director A. T. Smith told the *Washington Post*. "We train to the edge, and then we lean over." A final test in control tactics involves having two trainers jump each Secret Service agent candidate. The candidate must overcome them, unarmed. The president's Secret Service security detail trains two weeks out of every eight to stay refreshed and adapt to new threats.[5]

Sharp companies train too. They test their crisis management plans by doing crisis simulations to gauge how the plan holds up and how the crisis team performs in approximate real-life conditions. They also "media train" the company spokespeople, requiring them to handle mock press conferences, hostile media interviews, and critical online bloggers. The process is a continuous loop: the plans are revised continuously, simulations are conducted, and spokespersons are media trained regularly. Top companies make crisis management a key building block of their success and thereby improve their current operations and protect and preserve lives, resources, brands, and reputations.

Let me give you an example of how it works using a household brand name.

Syringes in Pepsi Cans?

In 1993, when Pepsi celebrated its ninety-fifth anniversary, Diet Pepsi was the number two diet drink in the country, and the company sold up to thirty million cans of its soft drinks a day.[6] On June 9 of that year, a Tacoma, Washington, couple reported finding a used syringe in a half-empty Diet Pepsi can. Within a week, consumers from twenty-three states made fifty additional claims of discovering syringes and other objects in Pepsi cans.[7] These product-tampering reports followed a rash of similar incidents that had occurred in the preceding decade, some with fatal consequences: Tylenol capsules laced with poison, rat poison in Contac cold medicine, glass fragments in Gerber baby food.

In the week after the June 9 report, Pepsi's stock sank and its sales of Diet Pepsi dropped 3–4 percent, representing millions of dollars in sales.[8] The media coverage spiked with each new reported incident, and Pepsi faced demands to recall its products. Pepsi confronted a classic beverage company nightmare: an assault on its brand and its reputation for providing safe soft drinks.

Pepsi's crisis management team had trained for product tampering scenarios and swung into high gear. Pepsi's CEO described the team's task: "Ensure consumer safety and security while protecting [Pepsi's] ninety-five-year-old trademark and maintaining a positive image amidst a blitz of often negative media attention."[9]

Here are some of the key moves the Pepsi crisis team made:

- Produced a video of its canning operations—blue and red cans whizzing by at 1,200 per minute—to demonstrate how difficult it would be to insert an object into a can.[10]

- Engineered a media blitz. Pepsi's CEO appeared on a dozen major TV shows, telling Larry King, "We are 99.99 percent certain that this didn't happen in Pepsi's plants."[11]

- Secured the FDA's support that a product recall was unnecessary and that there was no health risk from the tampering.[12]

- Circulated a store's surveillance camera video showing a woman trying to put a syringe into an open Pepsi can, which led to her felony arrest for tampering with the food supply.[13]

Scared by the threat of criminal prosecution, many consumers recanted their tales of tampering. Eight days after the first report, the crisis was over. Pepsi ran an ad in newspapers across the country stating it "was pleased to announce . . . nothing."[14]

Look at what Pepsi did. It had a crisis team ready to address product tampering. The team took charge of proving the tampering occurred outside its plants, assumed responsibility for fixing the problem, and enlisted the help of the FDA. The crisis team's work helped short-circuit a major threat to Pepsi's reputation and brand. Just like Morgan Stanley on 9/11, Pepsi followed the cardinal rule: "Plan the dive, dive the plan."

Instant Survivor™ Alert

You are now ready to do this in your life—you have a plan you can train for and follow—so you will take charge, get help, make smart moves, and put an end to trouble when it comes. Even though we know training is a key to survival in crisis situations, we often don't incorporate training into our lives.

MANAGER TIP #17—THE TRAINED SURVIVE

If you have a colleague who is suffering a personal or professional crisis, ask him or her this question:

Is there any training you could take to improve your ability to respond to the challenge in your life?

Have you practiced how you can escape from your house if there's a fire? Have you taken CPR training so you can rescue those around you? Have you taken self-defense training to avoid becoming a crime victim? Have you taken a course in the basics of financial planning? Do you know where the closest hospital is—both from your house and your office—in the event of an emergency? How about inviting your crisis management team over for a meal and running through possible scenarios: you lose your job, you get seriously injured, you face a financial setback. How about if each of your friends cites his or her own worst scenario, and each of you envisions practical steps to cover one another's backs?

Please take these steps. Inevitably you will find yourself in a distress situation. When that occurs, you will be reassured and confident because you have trained for trouble. Simply put, the trained survive.

•   •   •

Companies understand that crisis management plans are worthless without training. After all, what good is a plan if you are not able to follow it when you face a crisis? As an *Instant Survivor*™, you have to understand that training is the essential last step to saving your future.

As an *Instant Survivor*™, you must learn from your past without dwelling on it. Companies write after-action reports that they incorporate into their crisis management planning. They revise their plans with an emphasis on preserving their brand as

> **THE TRAINED SURVIVE**
>
> Preparation plus training produces peak performance.
>
> Train for trouble.
>
> Incorporate training into your life.

they conduct vulnerability audits to assess possible crisis points in the future. To save your future, you must define your brand and work hard to protect it. Your vulnerability audit will allow you to update your crisis management plan as you successfully navigate through your individual crises. Training will allow you to follow your plans more easily and develop the resilience you need to survive and thrive.

Now that you have completed the four-step crisis survival system, you will be able to follow the example of one woman who learned how to drive the bus when faced with trouble.

DRIVE, DON'T RIDE, THE BUS

On Memorial Day 2006, CBS News foreign correspondent Kimberly Dozier prepared to head out with a U.S. Army unit on patrol in Iraq. She showered, applied waterproof makeup, and put on her flak jacket. In the parking lot outside her hotel, she met her crew: cameraman Paul Douglas and soundman James Brolan. They all put in earplugs and pulled on helmets. They drove to the Green Zone for their 0800 rendezvous with U.S. Army Captain James Funkhouser Jr. and joined a convoy of four Humvees headed out to patrol several Baghdad neighborhoods. Dozier and her crew, along with Funkhouser and better than a dozen soldiers, stopped on a nearby street and stepped out of the vehicles to talk to residents.[1]

Kim's laser-like focus on becoming a TV network correspondent reflected her father's Marine credo: Put your head down, muscle through, don't complain. Repeat.[2] Her journey to the top had taken a personal toll; she was divorced, overworked, and frazzled by constant danger. Kim did not talk to her family about her fears and fatigue. Her father's tough-guy, bulldozer approach had a downside—family members rarely discussed emotional issues.

At thirty-nine years old, Kim felt she was where she wanted to be in her career and where she should be as a journalist.

Kim walked slightly behind Captain Funkhouser, an interpreter, and her crew as they moved in to speak with an Iraqi at a tea stand. As they neared the Iraqi, a three-hundred-plus-pound bomb concealed in a taxi detonated twenty feet away. The car bomb instantly killed Funkhouser, the interpreter, and Brolan. Within minutes, Douglas was also dead. Kim, laced with shrapnel, was nearly dead. An Iowa National Guardsman, whose unit happened to be nearby, performed CPR on her. She lost more than half her blood on the scene.

A Humvee transported her to a Green Zone hospital. Her survival prognosis on arrival was 50/50. Kim almost died five times on the operating table as doctors tried to stabilize her. Her right leg was broken in three places, her eardrum shattered.[3] When her producer arrived and saw her covered in blood, she thought Kim wouldn't make it.[4] A helicopter took Kim to a nearby airfield hospital for surgery to remove shrapnel from her skull. Next stop was a U.S. military hospital in Germany for severely injured soldiers. Here at this critical care facility, and later at the National Naval Medical Center in Bethesda, Maryland, the decisions Kim made—how well she managed her crisis—would determine whether she saved her life, her kidneys, and her sanity. Would Kim stand tall or crumble?

●   ●   ●

Let's stop right there. You're probably thinking, "Well, of the many things that might happen to me in my life, getting car-bombed in Iraq isn't one of them." And you're right. But while Kim's crisis started in a unique way, her struggle to work through a major trauma is something any of us could face, whether for an injury, disease, divorce, job loss, financial setback, or some other life upheaval.

Think about what you've learned so far. You appreciate that handling a crisis well means avoiding panic, sizing up a situation, and making a plan and implementing it.

If you were sitting at Kim's hospital bedside in Germany, what would you tell her? Would you suggest that she start gathering facts about her situation? How should she interact with her family, friends, and colleagues? How should she think about today, tomorrow, and her future? Would you quote to Kim the "live life for yourself" philosophy of ABC anchor Robin Roberts? That you need to focus on yourself to get past a disaster? Would you suggest she talk to others who have survived war injuries? Should she prepare a written plan when she's up to it? Most important, who would you tell her should be in charge of her recovery—her doctors, her family, or herself?

Let's see how Kim confronted her crisis.

Pain and Guilt

When Kim opened her eyes at Landstuhl Regional Medical Center in Germany, she immediately tried to talk but the tube down her throat made it impossible. She motioned for a pad of paper and started scribbling, but what she wrote was incomprehensible at first. She wanted to know what happened to her crew, first and foremost.[5] Then she told me she tried to link her memories into sequential order. She started with basic questions: "Where am I now? Where was I? What was the last thing that happened?" Because she was unconscious for a period after the blast and because the painkillers she was given had a memory-scrubbing effect, she had to struggle to piece together memories of the attack.

As Kim began to gather her memories, the doctors focused on saving her legs. They hammered rods into her leg bones so her legs would rotate properly in her hip sockets. Each day they put Kim under full anesthesia and power-washed dirt and dead tissue from her legs to set up future skin grafts.[6] Kim's mind shuffled between intense pain from broken bones and burns and worry over whether she would ever work or walk normally again.

Her principal nurse at Landstuhl wrote Kim a letter she could open when she was frustrated. It read, in part: "In your future lies more surgery, lots of rehab, hard work, and there will be frustration . . . look ahead to the bright future that awaits."[7]

Major General Mark Hertling, former second in command in Baghdad, slipped into her Landstuhl room to repeat to her what he had told injured troops: she should expect a long, painful rehabilitation and would have to cope with rugged self-examination because she survived while others had died. Hertling assured her, however, that with hard work and faith she could recover.[8]

Major General Hertling was right about the self-doubt that would set in for Kim. Besides her injuries, Kim was already confronting two inevitable aftermaths of the attack: grief and survivor's guilt.

Kim says her feelings ranged from sadness to anger when she understood what had happened to her. She says that she took time to grieve for herself and the other victims and feels fortunate she did. She has learned that trying to shortcut that process can keep a victim from making the full transition to becoming a survivor.

She says survivor's guilt is a powerful and potentially corrosive legacy of a deadly attack: the survivor blames herself and the families of the dead blame the survivor. Kim learned from grief counselors that this need to blame someone is a standard syndrome. She later spoke to the wife of Captain Funkhouser, who had learned from other war widows that after almost every attack there is blaming and recrimination. While at Landstuhl, Kim said her family lied to her; they told her that the families of her TV crew did not blame her for the attack. Later she learned that some family members believed it was her fault: she had pulled the crew into covering a needless story just so Kim could promote her career by getting on the air.

Family Dynamics

Kim says that shortly after the attack she replayed it "a thousand times in her head" and "thanked God over and over" that she hadn't come up with the story idea; it had been generated by CBS in New York. Injured ABC anchor Bob Woodruff also eased her guilt by reminding her that the cameraman and soundman were strong, independent guys who made their own decisions to go on the shoot. Woodruff told her, "If you think any differently, if you think of it any other way, you're dishonoring their memories."[9]

While essential to her own emotional recovery, Kim's desire to remember everything about the attack created a devastating tug-of-war between herself and her family and also her boyfriend, who had immediately rushed to her bedside in Landstuhl. They had all hoped that Kim would forget the violence. Understandably, her family wanted to protect her, not add to the overload of pain she was already suffering from her injuries.

Kim says her family also followed such old-fashioned rules as "don't talk about a problem" and "girls are weak." She says she wasn't told until months later—when CBS anchor Bob Schieffer visited her—that her heart had stopped five times on the operating table.

The "censorship" battle between Kim and her parents spilled over into how much they felt she should hear about her injuries. Her parents told the doctors not to give her negative information about her medical condition or outlook. While the doctors ignored these requests, Kim was furious when she heard about her family's cover-up efforts. "I didn't like liars. I didn't like people who would withhold information," she says. She felt like she had been through as much in her life as her parents had and that she was ready to hear the unvarnished facts.

Your Life or Your Kidneys

Kim spent a week in Landstuhl before she flew to Bethesda Naval Hospital. The Landstuhl medical report on Kim was positive: no brain damage and no need to amputate her right leg.

But at the time, Kim and the Landstuhl doctors didn't know that she was infected with *Acinetobacter baumannii*. Nicknamed Iraqi-bacter, the bacteria thrives in combat hospitals and is resistant to multiple drugs. When it infects a patient with a badly weakened immune system, like Kim, it can be fatal.

When Kim's trauma surgeon at Bethesda discovered her infection, he told her she was between a "rock and a hard place." Colistin, the only drug that could treat the bacteria, could also destroy her kidneys. Kim's family and her boyfriend immediately gathered medical research papers from around the United States, England, Israel, and New Zealand, trying to identify a safer way to attack the bacteria. There wasn't one. Kim started on a six-week course of colistin. Two weeks later, her blood tests showed signs of kidney failure.

A team of doctors arrived to tell her she had no choice but to stay on the colistin for the full six weeks to knock out the bacteria. They flatly said the drug would kill her kidneys and the next steps would be dialysis and a kidney transplant. The choice they presented to Kim was stark: lose her kidneys but kill the bacteria, or go off the colistin but risk the bacteria populating all of her body so that it caused organ failure and killed her. How could she stand tall when faced with such a predicament?

She and her surgeon debated the latter option: gamble and let her body fight the bacteria. If that didn't work, though, they'd have to try less effective means of combating it. After weighing the competing advice from the doctors, Kim took the risk. Fortunately, the two weeks she'd been on colistin had killed the bacteria, and her kidneys repaired themselves on their own.[10]

Struggling for Sanity

Kim says she spent a lot of time crying during the first few weeks after she arrived at Bethesda Naval. The combination of pain, guilt, and grief caused her to break down bawling throughout the day. The nurses knew it was part of the recovery process. They saw injured action-figure Marines regularly dissolving into tears in nearby rooms. But Kim's parents worried about her and wanted the hospital to help. Soon another medical debate raged: whether to give Kim antidepressants to address her fragile mental state or to let Kim rely on "talk therapy" to regain her emotional stability.

A hospital neuropsychiatrist told Kim to avoid talking about the attack. A team of visiting psychiatrists stopped by her room to offer drug therapy. They believed that drugs would lessen her emotional angst until the brain injury had healed, leaving her stronger to cope. But old military friends who'd been injured warned her that corking her pain and anger could lead to a mental breakdown. They advised her to talk to a therapist. Unfortunately, Bethesda Naval was short-staffed on that score.

Kim knew from her own experience that talking through problems was the right path. That's what she'd been doing as soon as the feeding tube was out of her mouth. She did not think she was cracking up. Surely the process of dredging up her memories and talking about them made her cry, yet she believed that was normal. She rejected the antidepressants.

In the last two weeks of her four-month stay at Bethesda Naval, a Navy Reservist psychologist rotated in. He confirmed the wisdom of her all-talk, no-drugs approach. The doc said Kim's tears were an appropriate response to her grief. He described how Marines and other soldiers in his care typically rebuffed his efforts to get them to open up about their feelings—an approach that left them alone with their tears.[11]

As Kim struggled with mental recovery, her physical setbacks continued. She had endured skin graft operations, transplanting healthy skin from her back and the top of her left leg to her right leg, which had taken the brunt of the blast. Her doctors later determined that the bandages covering these skin donor sites had trapped moisture. Rather than risk infection, they ripped off the bandages. The pain was excruciating, but got worse once the bandages were off and exposed the donor sites to air. Kim learned that no drug numbs skin pain, and Kim's plastic surgeon said the only treatment was to let the donor sites dry out, which could take up to a week. For the first time, Kim felt her grip on her sanity start to bend.

Desperate, Kim asked to see Bethesda's only wound nurse. Trained in the latest procedures for bandages and treatments, the nurse announced that the plastic surgeon's let-them-dry method was outdated. She directed the exact opposite treatment. She covered Kim's sites with clear film that protected the exposed nerves and kept the sites moist. Kim's pain relief was instant.[12]

Kim feared how her plastic surgeon would react. Her family had taught her that you listen to the ultimate authority, whether it was her father or a doctor. Kim's decision to follow the nurse's approach represented one of the few times she broke with this orthodoxy. Kim says, "I was presented with an option that preserved my sanity and I took it." Six weeks after the nurse's treatment started, the donor sites were healthy.

Family Fights

When Kim moved from Bethesda Naval to a rehabilitation facility near Baltimore, she says the battles with her parents got particularly ugly. They were upset when the doctors refused to give them a daily briefing on Kim's progress. Instead, the doctors informed them that they would brief Kim and she would decide how much to tell them. Her parents tried repeatedly to circumvent this protocol and extract information from the doctors. Kim and her parents had "screaming and shouting matches" about control of her treatment and the flow of information. She says several times she threw them out of her room. She felt her parents were trying to reestablish a parent-child relationship even though she was forty years old. She says she spent two-thirds of her time talking with counselors about how to deal with her family and one-third of her time talking about guilt, grief, and pain. A trauma counselor later told Kim that it is common for parents to revert to treating children who are adult trauma victims as they did before they left home.

Kim also learned that her boyfriend had been secretly calling CBS executives and telling them to withhold certain information from her because he said it was upsetting her. When Kim found out, she barred her parents and boyfriend from communicating with CBS and sent an e-mail to CBS executives thanking them for dealing with her family and friends, but advising them that if CBS needed to contact them, she would arrange it.

Kim says simply, "There are a lot of weird dynamics in rehabilitation and recovery."

Victim to Survivor

When Kim and I meet for lunch in Washington, DC, it is more than two and a half years after the bombing. She is casually dressed, with her strawberry blond hair pulled behind her ears. There is no sign of the car bombing in how she looks, acts, and speaks.

Kim is proud of what she has done as a survivor. She wrote an autobiography, *Breathing the Fire: Fighting to Report—and Survive—the War in Iraq.* She has given talks to military commanders and families so they will know what injured soldiers are going through. She is especially proud that she has shed light on the often-confused symptoms of post-traumatic stress (PTS) that, without treatment, can become the long-lasting post-traumatic stress disorder (PTSD).

Many people don't understand that it's natural for trauma victims to experience sleeplessness, flashbacks, irritability, and other symptoms in the first four to six weeks after an incident, as Kim did; that is called PTS. Her therapist believes she avoided developing PTSD by naturally engaging in exposure therapy, or as she puts it, by "talking her head off" about the incident. She recommends it for others. "If kids in the field are having nightmares and flashbacks after putting their buddies in body bags, it doesn't have to become PTSD if they talk about it and acknowledge it."

She is adamant about her transition from victim to survivor. She feels she has survived mentally, physically, and spiritually. But it's hard for family, friends, and colleagues to accept that she's fine and to remove her from "victim" status. A CBS executive wrote in an e-mail to Kim well after the attack, "I hope you're doing well or as well as can be expected." Kim fired back a photo of herself crossing the finish line at a recent Marine Corps 10K with the unspoken message, "Doing fine, thank you."

Time and distance from the hospitals and rehabilitation centers allow her to value more fully the critical roles her family and boyfriend played in her recovery. They researched her symptoms, analyzed her treatment options, advocated with the doctors, monitored her recovery, and loved her. While she butted heads with them about what she needed to know and her best treatment paths, she also knows they honestly felt she needed protection.

Kim celebrates her change as a person. She tells me she "was never as good as I am now." She says she was not a good listener before and feels she has gained empathy as a result of going through a horrible thing. "Now I listen to people and I feel what they're saying and it hurts."

She is philosophical about what traumatic experiences demand from people and how they will transform them. "Just understand the recovery process will be longer, slower, and likely more painful than you expected. But you will be a wiser and better person at the end of it. When I was little . . . I wanted to have this all-knowing understanding about what was going on around me. I wanted to advise other people." She laughed before continuing. "Had I known what it would take to get me there, I would have voted for dumb blonde."

Instant Survivor™ Alert

Kim is a poster child for successful crisis management and becoming an *Instant Survivor*™. Just by instinct, she implemented the four-step system described in this book. She stayed frosty, secured support, stood tall, and saved her future.

MANAGER TIP #18—PUTTING IT ALL TOGETHER

If you have a colleague who is suffering a personal or professional crisis, ask him or her this question:

Are you following a system to address your challenges?

Think how easy it is to be a passenger on a hospital bus ride designed by others. Meals arrive regularly. Friends and family dote on you. Nurses with clipboards give simple orders about when to take medication, when to turn over, when to go to the bathroom. Self-assured doctors announce treatment plans. But Kim understood that she was the driver of her recovery bus, and while her doctors, friends, and family had strong ideas, she had to direct her own recovery and make the

PUTTING IT ALL TOGETHER

Review the checklist of steps below. By observing each step, you will learn to drive, not ride, the bus when you face a crisis.

- Confront your fears and bring them into the light.
- Take personal charge of the situation.
- Gather accurate facts as quickly as possible.
- Acknowledge and voice your feelings about the crisis.
- Analyze the situation in an unemotional way.
- Focus on identifying the causes, symptoms, and cure for the crisis.
- Build a team around you to rely on, but restrain their efforts to overprotect or control you.
- Make decisions after getting the best advice possible from a range of people; experts aren't always right.
- Be selfish in pursuing a full recovery from victim to survivor.
- Focus on using the crisis to build a positive future for yourself and others.

important decisions that she would live with.

As soon as she opened her eyes in Landstuhl, she became the captain of her recovery. She stayed frosty. She started getting her bearings by coolly assessing her situation, asking questions of her family, friends, and doctors, and learning from visitors. Kim told me she "had this desperate need from the moment I opened my eyes to know every detail." She originally thought this was because of her background as a journalist, but she learned from trauma experts that part of the recovery process for trauma victims is to piece together what happened to them.

By being positive, energetic, and hardworking, Kim secured support by building a team around her that was dedicated to her recovery. At the same time, she did not deny her feelings: the intense grief and survivor's guilt. She "talked her head off" about the attack—what had happened and what it meant to her. She is convinced this enabled her to avoid the PTSD that cripples so many combat victims. Kim also started writing down her recollections of the incident and her reactions to it, eventually leading to her book. The writing process allowed her to work through her anger, sorrow, and pain and become a survivor with real perspective on her life.

She was "selfish" about focusing on her recovery, giving laser-like focus to getting the best advice and treatment. She broke down her recovery into small steps so she could celebrate many accomplishments along the way. She demanded honesty about the attack, her medical condition, and her prognosis; she put the brakes on her family and boyfriend, though, when she learned they were shielding her from the truth. Kim followed the classic effective crisis management approach: gather accurate facts and then make a careful analysis of the symptoms, causes, and cure for the crisis.

Effective crisis management requires making good decisions under pressure with incomplete or conflicting information. Here, Kim stood remarkably tall. Remember the hard, critical decisions she made about how to fight off potentially fatal bacteria, address her sadness, and avoid infection in her skin graft sites. She listened to her doctors, nurses, and family, and her own instincts. In the face of raging medical and family debates, she selected treatment paths that enabled her to save her life, her kidneys, and her sanity.

Kim also used the attack in a positive way to build a better future for herself and others. She shared the knowledge she had gained as a combat survivor with the military and families of wounded soldiers. She became a better listener. She committed herself to a life of spreading the truth and living with honor.

• • •

Kim Dozier demonstrated an almost supernatural ability to deal with an almost unimaginable crisis. Not all of us have Kim's strength, but we all have the ability to become Instant Survivors.

CONCLUSION

In Roman mythology, the god Janus rules beginnings and transitions. He has two heads, which face opposite directions: one eastward, one westward. Symbolically his heads look simultaneously into the future and the past, back at the last year and forward to the new one.[1]

Let's pretend we are Janus-faced for a moment so we can simultaneously examine your past and peer into your future.

Of course, standard life advice from as far back as the Bible tells us not to look back. Lot's wife looked back at Gomorrah and was reduced to a pillar of salt. Modern wise men have chimed in with similar instructions. Baseball pitcher Satchel Paige warned, "Don't look back, something might be gaining on you." Author Eckhart Tolle writes, "I have little use for the past and rarely think about it."[2]

When it comes to disasters, we know this advice is wrong. Only the melodramatic among us experience crises as exciting, unpredictable, and even thrilling events. Most of us find these adverse situations debilitating, paralyzing, and maddening; only the insane would want to repeat them. Spanish-American philosopher George Santayana, who taught philosophy at Harvard to such wise men as poet Robert Frost and journalist Walter Lippmann, got it right: "Those who cannot remember the past are condemned to repeat it."[3]

If you have just come through a crisis, use your Janus head to look back. See what you did well. See what you'd like to improve. See how you can prevent future crises.

Some of this book may have struck a particular chord with you, some not. You may have done some of the exercises, skipped others. Remind yourself what worked for you. Is it using paper to map a response to a catastrophe? Is it accepting that you should be selfish to survive? Is it appreciating your need to stay visible when troubles arrive? Your individual psyche and your particular crisis are each unique as snowflakes; shape your response to your situation in a way that works for you.

Isabel Gillies, the TV actor whose husband left her for another woman, wants to make sure her new marriage stays intact, so she gets professional help to look back and learn how she might have contributed to the dissolution of her first marriage. TV anchor Robin Roberts consults a nutritionist to help ward off a return of her cancer. Former U.S. Senator Max Cleland seeks regular counseling for his post-traumatic stress disorder to prevent a recurrence of depression.

Now let's look forward. A recent *New Yorker* magazine cartoon pictured a long-faced woman sitting across from a fortune-teller who was peering into a crystal ball. The fortune-teller advised her: "You will make the same foolish mistakes you have made before, not only once but many, many times again."[4] That won't be you.

The crystal ball shows that you are now free. Free from the worry that you can't handle a crisis. Free from the dread that accompanies an upheaval. Free from the insistent "inner voice" that tells you, "You don't know what to do," "This one is too big for you to handle," and "You're going to get crushed."

A Norwegian maxim reminds us that it's easy to be a good captain in a calm sea. You are now equipped to calm the sea of your life, but also to navigate around and through the storms and waves that will inevitably surface. You are now trained to survive.

Of course, you'll continue to be tested, pressed, and stressed, but you are different now. Your brand is stronger. Your safety net is solid. Your vulnerability audit of your life reassures you. You have identified weaknesses and shored them up before trouble hits. You have your radar up to spot distant trouble and resolve it before it capsizes you and your loved ones. You are at the controls of your life.

You will react differently to trouble. You have in place a crisis management plan. By following it, you will unfreeze your brain, ask good questions, gather facts, be guided by your crisis management team, take smart steps, make sound decisions under stress, and conquer whatever crisis you face, personal or professional.

How can you take advantage of your accomplishment of becoming a skilled crisis manager? How is your life better?

Breathe more easily. Lift your gaze higher. Embrace life with renewed confidence, purpose, and joy. Live more boldly. Take more risks. Follow your dreams. Stay true to yourself, to your calling, to your faith.

You will save yourself and others who depend on you. Saving others brought Captain "Sully" Sullenberger a torrent of mail from well-wishers after the safe water landing of Flight 1549. Here is what one Manhattan resident wrote him: "Had you not been so skilled, my father or others like him in their sky-high buildings could have perished along with your passengers. As a Holocaust survivor, my father taught me that to save a life is to save a world, as you never know how the person you saved, nor his or her prodigy, will go on to contribute to the peace and healing of the world."[5]

By saving yourself and others, you will contribute to the peace and healing of the world. Why wait? Let's get to it!

ACKNOWLEDGMENTS

Writing this book evolved into a saga. Navigating the complexities and storms of the publishing world required a navy of professionals, friends, and family. They directed me through the tumult—with guidance, encouragement, and love.

To my wife, Gillian, my daughter, Nini, and my son, Will: you are the most thrilling thing that has happened to me in my life and always will be, and I love you and treasure your love. To my mother, Lucy, and my siblings, Bill, Penny, and Steve: your love, hysterical sense of humor, and wonderfully positive example set my course from before my first steps. I love you. To my father: we miss your love, courage, and support.

To my special friends who blessed this book with their interest, prodding, questions, and enthusiasm, thank you: Susan Moorhead, John Leboutillier, Will Schwartz, John Dodderidge, David Cook, Suzi Pomerantz, Paige Lichens, Kim Davis, Shawn Edgington, Taryn Davis and the American Widow Project, Christine Eisner, Molly Blythe Teichert, Brendon Burchard, Teri Hawkins, my QL and SEC buddies, Steve and Bill Harrison, Sam Horn, Amanda Deaver, Charles Bakaly, Denise Brosseau, and Geoff Berwind.

To Greenleaf Book Group: you embraced me and this book with your dedication, imagination, and professionalism. A special thanks to Tanya Hall, Bill Crawford, and Julie Prien.

To my colleagues at my firm: your brains, commitment, and enthusiasm transform every day.

To my TMG clients and the thousands of people who've attended my presentations, read my blog, and will read this book: You have honored me by inviting me into your lives. I will work to keep your trust. Contact me at jim@instantsurvivor.com if you have any questions. I will get back to you.

Finally, my appreciation and admiration flow to all those brave survivors of professional and personal crises whom I interviewed for the book and all others whose stories fill these pages. Your honesty and insights enlarged and inspired me—and I hope many others.

ENDNOTES

1   Jeffrey Zaslow, "New Index Aims to Calculate the Annual Cost of Despair," *Wall Street Journal*, November 20, 2002.
2   Donna St. George, "Estranged Spouses Increasingly Waiting Out Downturn to Divorce," *Washington Post*, March 22, 2010, p. B1.
3   Anne Tergesen, "Sending Out an Elder-Care SOS," *Wall Street Journal*, March 5, 2011.
4   "Caregiving in the U.S.," Executive Summary, National Alliance for Caregiving in Collaboration with AARP, November 2009.

Chapter One
1   Isabel Gillies, *Happens Every Day* (New York: Scribner, 2009).
2   Ibid., p. 256.
3   Amanda Ripley, *The Unthinkable* (New York: Three Rivers Press, 2008), pp. 8-9.

Chapter Two
1   Robin Roberts, *From the Heart: Eight Rules to Live By* (New York: Hyperion, 2007), p. 167

Chapter Three
1   Diane Rehm, *Finding My Voice* (Vermont: Capital Books, 1999), pp. 189–90.
2   Ibid., pp. 193–95.
3   Ibid., pp. 206–09.
4   Ibid., pp. 220–21.
5   James E. Lukaszewski, "Telling the Truth Reduces Liability, Who Woulda Thought?" PBI Media LLC *PR News*, April 17, 2000.
6   John M. Barry, "Pandemics: Avoiding the Mistakes of 1918," *Nature*, May 21, 2009.
7   "Know Yourself, Know Your Rival," *USA Today*, July 20, 2009, p. 3B.
8   "Homeowners Let Emotions Drive Decisions to Default," *Wall Street Journal*, May 11, 2010, p. A5.

9   "For Gen Y Woman with Cancer Risk, 'It's Just a Boob,'" CNN.com, 2009.

10   "Healing with Humor," *Washington Post*, July 27, 2009, p. A1.

Step Two

1   Nathaniel Fick, *One Bullet Away: The Making of a Marine Officer* (Boston: Houghton Mifflin, 2005), p. 29.

Chapter Four

1   Wikipedia, quoting 1972 interview of Kissinger by Oriana Fallaci, accessed May 22, 2011.

2   Catherine Bergart, "Losing the Income, and the Camaraderie," *New York Times*, May 17, 2009.

3   Benedict Carey, "The After-Life of Near Death," *The New York Times*, January 18, 2009.

4   Daniel J. Sertowitz and Sue Schultz, "Feeling Blue?," *Baltimore Business Journal*, November 14–20, 2008.

5   Max Cleland, *Heart of a Patriot* (New York: Simon & Schuster, 2009), p. 79.

6   Max Cleland, *Strong at the Broken Places* (Vermont: Chosen Books), pp. 65–6.

7   Dionne Searcey, "Post-Madoff, a Support Network," *The Wall Street Journal*, February 2, 2009, p. C3.

8   "Anguish over California Teen Suicides Spurs Action," Lisa Leff, Associated Press, 2009.

9   Laura Landro, "After Cancer Diagnosis, A Mentor," *Wall Street Journal*, October 27, 2009, p. B9.

10   Elizabeth Weise, "Online Bonds of Parenthood," *USA Today*, June 22, 2010, p. D10.

11   Jeff Trusdell, "A Lot More Living To Do," *People*, December 13, 2010, p. 82.

12   Dr. Phil McGraw, "We Can Get Through This Together," *Parade*, May 17, 2009, p. 8.

13   Harriet Brown, "Coping with Crises Close to Someone Else's Heart," *New York Times*, August 18, 2010.

Chapter Five

1   Lawrence G. McDonald and Patrick Robinson, *A Colossal Failure of Common Sense: The Inside Story of the Collapse of Lehman Brothers* (New York: Crown Business 2009).

2   Jason Zweig, "Wall Street Lays Eggs with Its Nest Eggs," *Wall Street Journal*, September 27, 2008.

3   http://wealthmediation-uwwm.blogspot.com, accessed September 11, 2011.

4   Randy Jackson, *Body With Soul*, (London: Hudson Street Press, 2008), pp. xiii–xiv.

5   Jim Roberts, "Biggest Loser Winner Ali Vincent Speaks Out, Gives Tips," *National Ledger*, April 18, 2008.
6   Michelle Tan, "I'm Sick of Being Big," *People*, June 22, 2009, pp. 100–106.
7   Quoted at www.justinseasonaltreasures.com/quotes/dmacarthur.php; accessed May 22, 2011.

Chapter Six
1   Geoff Colvin, "The Upside of the Downturn," CNNMoney.com, May 28, 2009.
2   Ted Rowlands, "Blogging Begins Turnaround for Homeless Woman," www.CNN.com/2009/LIVING/09/11/homeless.blogger/index.html.
3   Quoted at www.nps.gov/history/logcabin/html/vf.html accessed on May 22, 2011.
4   "Paine's Echoes," James J. Donnelly.com.
5   Quoted in www.positiveleadershiplimited.blogspot.com, accessed October 6, 2009.

Chapter Seven
1   Lorraine Woellert and Yalman Onaran, "Fuld Blames Lehman's Fall on Rumors, 'Storm of Fear,'" Bloomberg.com, visited October 6, 2008.
2   Graham Bowley, "Taking Spin Out for a Spin," *New York Times*, November 22, 2009.
3   "Another View: Who's Sorry Now?," *New York Times*, January 7, 2010.
4   Ruben Castaneda, "Charles Judge Says Deflating Tire Wasn't a 'Big Deal,' His Supervisor Says," *Washington Post*, August 13, 2009.
5   "Vigilante Judge Deflates Tire of Court Employee: Judges Are Vengeful, TOO!!," Legallyunbound.com, August 13, 2009.
6   Ruben Casteneda, "Md. Judge Who Deflated Tire Calls Actions 'Calculated,'" *Washington Post*, April 29, 2010.
7   Ruben Casteneda and Christy Goodman, "Judge Is Suspended from Criminal Cases," *Washington Post*, August 15, 2009.
8   Ibid.
9   Colin Woodard, "A Quiet Apology," *Down East*, August 2010.
10 Quoted at www.bernsteincrisismanagement.com, accessed November 25, 2009.
11 "Did Gibson's Apology Come Too Late?," Associated Press, msnbc.com, accessed November 25, 2009.
12 "Officials Reviewing Serena's Actions," ESPN.com, accessed May 17, 2011.
13 Bill Dwyre, "Serena's Ugly Outburst Deserves Lengthy Spill on the Sidelines," theage.com, accessed May 18, 2011.
14 "Officials Reviewing Serena's Actions," ESPN.com, accessed May 17, 2011.

15   Bonnie Ford, "Serena: 'I Want to Sincerely Apologize,'" ESPN.com, September 14, 2009, accessed May 18, 2011.

16   Emily Dugan, "The $50 Trick (or How Divine Brown Turned an Encounter with Hugh Grant into Her Fortune)," *The Independent*, July 3, 2007.

17   Bernard Weinraub, "What's the Hollywood Topic? Hugh Grant's Future, Mainly," *New York Times*, June 29, 1995.

18   "*Nine Months* Star Hugh Grant Runs Talk Show Gauntlet," CNN.com, July 11, 1995.

19   Andrea Sachs, "The New World of Crisis Management," TIME.com, April 19, 2007.

20   "Human Frailty Caused This Crisis," FT.com, November 12, 2008.

21   Jane J. Kim, "Corporate Mea Culpas Shown to Pay," *Wall Street Journal*, April 21, 2004, p. B4D.

Chapter Eight

1   Dale Carnegie, *How to Stop Worrying and Start Living* (New York: Pocket Books, 1944), pp. 36–39.

2   Michael J. Cain, "Therapeutic Journaling Promotes Healing," Army News Service, April 27, 2010.

3   Atul Gawande, *The Checklist Manifesto* (New York: Metropolitan Books/ Henry Holt & Company), 2009.

4   Ceci Connolly, "Surgery Checklist Lowers Death Rate," *Washington Post*, January 15, 2009, p. A2.

5   Dan Barry, "Living in Tents, and by the Rules, Under a Bridge," *New York Times*, July 31, 2009.

6   Michael J. Cain, "Therapeutic Journaling Promotes Healing," Army News Service, April 27, 2010.

Chapter Nine

1   Gretchen Morgenson, "Was There a Loan It Didn't Like?," *New York Times*, November 2, 2008.

2   Frank Pellegrini, "Person of the Week: 'Enron Whistleblower' Sherron Watkins," *TIME*, January 18, 2002.

3   Alexi Barrionuevo, "Warning on Enron Is Recalled," *New York Times*, March 16, 2006.

4   "John Edwards Extramarital Affair," Wikipedia, accessed February 20, 2011.

5   "Indulgence," *New Yorker*, April 19, 2010, p. 31.

6   Mollie Ziegler Hemingway, "More Emphasis on Confessing Might Have Helped," *Wall Street Journal*, June 4, 2010, p. W9.

7   "Abuse Crisis Strains Vatican's Ancient Ways of Management," *New York Times*, April 6, 2010.

8   "Catholics in Crisis," *The Week*, May 7, 2010, p. 11.

9   Vanessa Gera, "Catholics Find Ties to the Church Tested by Crisis," Associated Press, 2010.

10 "Catholics in Crisis," *The Week*, May 7, 2010, p. 11.

11 "Pat Tillman," Wikipedia, accessed February 20, 2011.

12 "Dick Cheney Hunting Incident," Wikipedia, accessed February 20, 2011.

13 Aliyah Shahid, "Dick Cheney Shooting Victim, Harry Whittington, Doesn't Dispute that Ex-VP Never Apologized," *New York Daily News*, October 14, 2010.

14 Michael Isikoff, "The Fed Who Blew the Whistle," *Newsweek*, December 13, 2008.

Chapter Ten

1   David Wessel, "Government's Trial and Error Helped Stem Financial Panic," *Wall Street Journal*, September 4, 2009.

2   "Apollo 13 . . . ' A Problem,'" http://history.nasa.gov/apollo/app13.html, accessed February 26, 2011.

3   Margaret J. King, Ph.D., "Failure Is Not an Option: Apollo 13 Creativity," *R&D Innovator*, vol. 5, no. 9, September 1996.

4   Andrew Chalkin, "Apollo 13 Mission Log Day 5: Expect the Unexpected," Space.com, accessed December 1, 2008.

5   Rick Amme, "Coping with the Unexpected: The U.S. Marines' Approach," Bernsteincrisismanagement.com, accessed November 21, 2007.

6   "Nobelists to Students: Being Wrong May Just Be Right," *Science News*, July 4, 2009.

7   Sean Wilentz, "The Worst President in History?," *Rolling Stone*, April 21, 2006.

8   Ibid.

9   E. J. Dionne Jr., Quoted in "Roosevelt, America's Original Man from Hope," *Washington Post*, May 1, 1997.

10 Amy Merrick and Roger Thurow, "The Jobless Go Back to School and, They Hope, Work," *Wall Street Journal*, February 5, 2009.

11 Brainyquote.com, accessed May 17, 2011.

Chapter Eleven

1   Peggy Noonan, "To-Do List: A Sentence, Not 10 Paragraphs," *Wall Street Journal*, June 27–28, 2009.

2   http://www.uncg.edu/bcn/eddedward/204/unit2/tv_ppt.html, accessed September 13, 2011.

3   http://marketingstudio.net/2010/04/08/crisis-communications-new-standard, accessed August 14, 2011.

Chapter Twelve

1   Mark Levine, "High Hurdles," *Runner's World*, December 2009.

2   Ibid., pp. 92–93.

3   Ibid., p. 93.

4   Ibid., p. 107.

5   Lee Child, "My Good Life After Being Fired," *Parade*, June 26, 2009.

6   David Koller, "Laid-off lawyer decides to start a solo career," *Legal Intelligencer*, November 25, 2009.

7   Bryan Nichols, "Check Your Bags—and Fear—at the Gate," *Maryland Bar Bulletin*, February 2009.

8   Nicholas D. Kristof, "Not A Victim, But a Hero," *New York Times*, July 26, 2009.

9   Dorothy Markulis, "Resident Turns Medical Crisis into Business Helping Others," *Hudson Hub Times*.

10 Kari Lydersen, "Paralympic Offer Wounded Veterans a Chance to Dream," *Washington Post*, August 9, 2009, p. A7.

11 Howard Stock, "Baseball Hero Puts Up Good Numbers at La. Bank," *American Banker*, November 6, 2008, p. 9.

12 Bryan Ruiz Switsky, "Investing in the Downturn," *Washington Business Journal*, November 14–20, 2008, p. 37.

13 Debra Cassens Weiss, "Associate Laid Off Twice in Four Months Looks at the Bright Side," AmericanBarJournal.com, 2009.

14 Jessica Mulvihill, "20 Years After Attack, 'Central Park Jogger' Offers Hope," FOXNews.com, 2009.

15 Amy Cohen, "Just Go Forward," *Wesleyan Magazine*.

16 Viktor E. Frankl, *Man's Search for Meaning* (Boston: Beacon Press, 1959), p. 75.

17 Ibid., p. 87.

18 Ibid., p. 84.

19 "A New View, After Diagnosis," Melinda Beck, *Wall Street Journal*, July 14, 2009, p. D1.

Chapter Thirteen

1   Mark Stuertz, "Foundation of Hope," *American Way*, February 1, 2010, p. 27.

2   http://dineidert.wordpress.com/tag/commitments, accessed September 11, 2011.

3   www.personalbrandingblog.com/4-step-personal-brand-promise-checklist, accessed September 16, 2011.

4   http://www.broqueville.com/documents/Volume1_Session48.pdf, accessed September 18, 2011.

Chapter Fourteen

1   Scott M. Davis, *Brand Asset Management,* John Wiley & Sons, 2002, p. 3.

2   Ray George, "Achieving Consistency—Delivering on Your Brand Promise Across All Customer Touchpoints," Prophet.com, accessed May 21, 2011.

3   www.brandreputation.com, accessed May 21, 2011.

4   http://www.religare.com/brandidentity.aspx, accessed September 19, 2011.

5   www.jnj.com, accessed May 22, 2011.

6   Christopher S. Tang, "Making Products Safe: Process and Challenges," ProQuest Information and Learning, *ECR Journal International Commerce Review,* Autumn, 2008.

7   Michael Holley, *Red Sox Rule: Terry Francona and Boston's Rise to Dominance* (New York: HarperCollins, 2008), pp. 70–71.

8   Tom Peters, "The Brand Called You," Fastcompany.com, http://www.fastcompany.com/node/28905/print, accessed September 16, 2011.

9   http://personalbrandingblog.wordpress.com/2008/11/03/can-you-list-your-personal-brand, accessed September 16, 2011.

10 Tom Peters, "The Brand Called You," Fastcompany.com, http://www.fastcompany.com/node/28905/print, accessed September 16, 2011.

11 Brandandreputation.com, accessed August 14, 2011.

12 http://personalbrandingblog.wordpress.com/2008/11/03/can-you-list-your-personal-brand, accessed September 16, 2011.

13 http://deluxesmallbizblog.com/wp-content/uploads/2011/03/The-Essential-Branding-Checklist.pdf, accessed August 14, 2011.

Chapter Fifteen

1   "Business Continuity Checklist (Insurance for Your Business)," http:/blog.fibertown.com, accessed May 17, 2011.

2   Richard S. Levick, "They Were Ready' . . .BP's Orange County Spill Response Remains the Industry Standard for Public Crisis Management," *Mealey's Emerging Toxic Torts,* 2004.

Chapter Sixteen

1   http://iam-bc.com/blog/are-you-autopilot-work, accessed September 19, 2001.

2   Charles Volkert, "Is Your Job in Trouble?" http://www.lawyeravenue.com/2008/04/22/is-your-job-in-trouble-2, accessed September 16, 2011.

3   Sheryl Nance-Nash, "The 100-Day Turnaround," *Arrive Magazine,* January/February 2009, p. 32.

4   Quoted at www.thinkexist.com/quotation/there_is_no_dignity_quite_
    so_impressive-and_no/1163167.html., accessed May 22, 2011.
5   "Ed McMahon Explains His Mortgage Mess," CNN Entertainment, June 6,
    2008, http://articles.cnn.com, accessed May 17, 2011.
6   Jason Zweig, "Wall Street Lays Egg with Its Nest Eggs," *Wall Street Journal*,
    September 27, 2008.
7   Dr. Ranit Mishori, "Who Gets Sick in America—and Why," *Parade*, June
    28, 2009.

Chapter Seventeen
1   Michael Grunwald, "A Tower of Courage," *Washington Post*, October 28,
    2002; author's interview with Susan Rescorla.
2   James B. Stewart, *Heart of a Soldier* (New York: Simon & Schuster, 2002).
3   Michael Grunwald, "A Tower of Courage," *Washington Post*, October 28,
    2002.
4   Ben Sherwood, *The Survivors Club* (New York: Grand Central Publishing,
    2009), pp. 210-14.
5   Laura Blumenfeld, "The Making of an Agent," *Washington Post*, July 26,
    2009.
6   "Effective Communication," Brainmass.com, accessed February 21,
    2009; "The Diet-Pepsi Crisis," Newsflavor.com, March 9, 2008; Michael
    Janofsky, "Reports of Needles in Soda Cans Climb," *New York Times*, June
    16, 1993.
7   Betty Mohr, "The Pepsi Challenge: Managing a Crisis," Findarticles.com,
    accessed February 21, 2009.
8   "Effective Communication," Brainmass.com, accessed February 21, 2009.
9   Betty Mohr, "The Pepsi Challenge: managing a crisis," March 1994
    Findarticles.com, accessed February 21, 2009.
10 "Effective Communication," Brainmass.com, accessed February 21, 2009.
11 Betty Mohr, "The Pepsi Challenge: managing a crisis," March 1994,
    Findarticles.com, accessed February 21, 2009.
12 "Effective Communication," Brainmass.com accessed February 21, 2009.
13 "The Diet-Pepsi Crisis," Newsflavor.com, March 9, 2008.
14 "Effective Communication," Brainmass.com, accessed February 21, 2009.

Putting It All Together
1   Kim Dozier, *Breathing the Fire* (Des Moines: Meredith Books, 2008),
    pp. 9–17.
2   Ibid., p. 135.

3   Peter Johnson, "'Flashpoint' Tells the Story of Wounded CBS Reporter Dozier," *USA Today*, May 24, 2007; Felicia R. Lee, "One Bomb, 25 Operations and 363 Days to Return to TV," *New York Times*, May 24, 2007.

4   Kim Dozier, *Breathing the Fire*, p. 53.

5   Ibid., pp. 18–22.

6   Ibid., pp. 77–78, 126.

7   Ibid., p. 95–96.

8   Ibid., p. 87.

9   Felicia R. Lee, "One Bomb, 25 Operations and 363 Days to Return to TV," *New York Times*, May 24, 2007.

10 Kimberly Dozier, *Breathing the Fire*, pp. 158–64.

11 Ibid., pp. 179–83.

12 Ibid., pp. 200–207.

Conclusion

1   "Janus," Wikipedia, accessed May 21, 2011.

2   Eckhart Tolle, *The Power of Now* (Novato, CA: New World Library, 1999), p. 3.

3   The Santayana Edition, http://www.inpui.edu, accessed May 17, 2011.

4   Gahan Wilson, *New Yorker*, January 18, 2010.

5   Andrea Doyle, "Captain Sullenberger's Miracle on the Hudson," November 2, 2010, Successfulmeeting.com, accessed May 20, 2011.

MEET JIM MOORHEAD

What began as a knack for helping friends, family members, and class-mates through personal struggles has grown into a lifelong career for Jim Moorhead, America's crisis advisor. Jim's humanity and passion for showing others how to confidently navigate through difficult situations is nothing short of remarkable.

Jim underwent his own personal crisis when he lost a statewide race that would have launched his political career. A few years later he accepted an extremely promising job, but the dot-com bust drove him even deeper into crisis. Drawing from a career spent helping corporations overcome large-scale upheavals, Jim developed a simple, actionable four-step system to help himself—and others—clear the types of professional and personal hurdles that many individuals encounter during their lives.

A graduate of Harvard College and Columbia Law School, Jim has coached hundreds of employees, business leaders, and political can-didates on how to confront and conquer professional and personal disasters. An inspiring speaker as well as a respected crisis advisor, Jim regularly provides commentary on business and legal crises and has appeared on CNN, CNBC, MSNBC, *Fox News, Fox Business, Court TV,* and *America's Talking.*

Jim's work history as a reporter, investment banker, federal pros-ecutor, and political candidate gives him a breadth of experience that enables him to tailor his crisis management advice to individuals in all fields. He is currently a partner at a major Washington, DC, law firm, where he cofounded and cochairs the company's crisis management practice. With *The Instant Survivor: Right Ways to Respond When Things Go Wrong*, Jim has written *the* book on personal and professional crisis management and has become one of the country's most sought-after crisis management speakers.

It's Time to Create Your Own Instant Survivor Handbook!

Thanks for reading *The Instant Survivor*. It is my sincere hope that it will serve you well in future crisis situations. While some say that we are all survivors, we know from experience that those who prepare for crisis situations have a much better chance of getting through them successfully.

To help you create your own personalized resource, I created *The Instant Survivor*™ Handbook, which is filled with action items, tips, and other resources to help you think about how you can survive any crisis that may stand in your way.

It is available for free download at
www.instantsurvivor.com

Once you complete your *Instant Survivor*™ Handbook, please let me know if it serves you well in the future.